To Minister
His Grace

STUART THOMAS is an anglican priest and vicar of St. Francis of Assisi at Ewell in Surrey. He has been involved in the church's healing ministry for many years and was a member of Guildford Christian Healing Group which organized conferences on healing under the leadership of Francis MacNutt. He himself has led conferences on the subject both in this country and in Germany, (his degree in German and Russian from Pembroke College, Cambridge proving useful there!). He is a member of the Guildford Diocesan Worship Committee and speaks regularly at conferences on liturgy and music in worship.

The author of *God with us, Keep it in the Family, Christian Services for Schools* and *Confirmation to Follow*, (all published by Kevin Mayhew), Stuart Thomas's main hobbies are music (he is an accomplished pianist), and collecting toy cars.

To Minister His Grace
Healing Services for the Church

Stuart Thomas

Kevin
Mayhew

First published in 1995 by
KEVIN MAYHEW LTD
Rattlesden
Bury St Edmunds
Suffolk IP30 0SZ

ISBN 0 86209 646 4
Catalogue No 1500024

Front cover: *Peacock Garden* designed by Walter Crane.
Reproduced by kind permission of Victoria & Albert Museum,
London/Bridgeman Art Library, London.
Cover design by Graham Johnstone

Typesetting and Page Creation by Vicky Brown
Printed and bound in Great Britain.

CONTENTS

INTRODUCTION

L IKE ANY other part of society the Church is liable to have an occasional fad for something. For a while a great deal of energy is expended on the activity in question, only for something else to come on the scene a little while later and draw on the well of enthusiasm. Judging by the number of churches who would now claim to have some kind of healing ministry as a normal part of their everyday life, healing services are rapidly becoming 'de rigueur'. Some will view this as a very positive development, basing their outlook both on the Bible and the Christian tradition, while others respond much more cautiously, even sceptically. There will be differences too on how this ministry should be exercised, and even on who should exercise it. Sadly, conflict has at times been generated within a particular church over the question of Christian healing, resulting in a situation which is far from healthy and in relationships which need healing. As with most conflicts, there is plenty of scope for addressing the issues involved without bad feeling or damaged friendships. Provided that everyone is familiar with the basic information, Christian healing need not cause more strife than any other part of the church's ministry.

Most churches will find in their congregation a number of folk who react anxiously and defensively at the prospect of an innovation that seems over-emotional and 'untraditional. They want to preserve the church's traditions and heritage, but they may well have heard a few 'horror stories' from friends or even the media. One or two may themselves have had a bad experience of an ill-conceived or obviously manipulated healing event. On the other hand, there will also be a number who feel very positively towards the Christian healing ministry because their own experience of it has been good, or they know someone else who has found it beneficial.

This book makes no attempt to 'sell' the Christian healing ministry or the idea of healing services; in fact, you probably picked it up because you're sympathetic to the concept. It has two basic aims:

i to give some background information and practical help to enable churches to understand better the nature of Christian healing, and to practise it in a helpful and non-threatening way.

ii to provide a selection of resource material which can be used in healing services, and some outline liturgies which can be adapted to particular local situations and needs.

One of the most frequent causes of opposition to the healing ministry of the Church is the failure to introduce it with sensitivity or care. If it becomes the preserve of a group who are seen as 'extremists' or if it arrives on the scene without prior warning or teaching, there will soon be antagonism and conflict. By the same token, if well handled, the healing ministry will be absorbed without difficulty into the church's life and people will be drawn to it who otherwise would have steered well clear. It is true that many churches do now include it as a regular part of their ministry, but there is no point in doing so simply because it is the 'in thing'. Everyone needs to understand its nature and aims, and recognise the potential pitfalls if it is to fulfil its role properly.

There are two parts to this book. The first takes a look at what we mean by healing, and fits that into the context of both the witness of the Bible and the history and traditions of the church. It also covers different ways in which people can be healed and how we might go about praying for them. That provides the necessary background for a discussion of healing services and how to conduct them. The second part provides a compendium of resources that might be used in the context of a formal liturgy. There is not a prescription which will fit every church and situation. While the principles form a framework within which a healing service can be planned, you will need to interpret and adapt the material to your own local circumstances, which might include tradition, architecture, musical and other resources, as well as a wide range of sensitivities! I hope and pray that it will make its own contribution to the spread of the Christian healing ministry.

PRINCIPLES

WHAT IS HEALING?

FEW SOCIETIES can have been more obsessed with the human body and its health than our own. Wherever we look we find an avalanche of advice about caring for ourselves not just physically but mentally and spiritually too. No self-respecting magazine is without a couple of pages from various experts on topics ranging from heart conditions and warts to chronic depression and retirement. The problems of coping with adolescence need hold no terrors for those who read the right columns or books, and all the answers are apparently there if you need to know about caring for elderly relatives when they become infirm. And no relationships are likely to cause difficulties for long if you follow what is suggested. Even in the relatively small market for Christian literature there is no end to the good counsel available on these and many other issues which concern us at various stages of our lives. In fact, most of us think we are experts ourselves on medical and psychological problems, because there are so many books available to inform us and make us aware. Volumes such as 'Families and how to survive them' or 'The Hip and Thigh Diet' are predictable bestsellers, while books on correct eating could fill several shelves of anyone's library. I long ago came to the conclusion that if we followed every bit of dietary advice on what not to eat, we would probably die of starvation instead!

What has brought about this extreme concern with matters of health and fitness? Surely every society has had to face these issues? Human beings have always had to cope with life and death, but in the last few years medical technology has made quite astonishing advances. Illnesses and conditions which were formerly regarded as incurable are no longer feared and 'spare part surgery' has now become commonplace. I well remember Professor Christian Barnard becoming a celebrity when he performed the first heart transplant less than 30 years ago. Nowadays the only factor preventing this becoming fairly routine seems to be the cost. And while most of us may not need such radical treatment, we all benefit from the vast array of medication now on the market. As a result we live longer and like to think we are more in control of our destiny.

I would not want to create the wrong impression, however. I am all in favour of good health care, and if I am feeling off-colour I go to see the doctor and take whatever treatment he prescribes. I certainly do not take the view that the Christian healing ministry is in permanent conflict with the National Health Service. God has created all things, including our bodies and the substances that can make them well, and while I have seen him override the usual rules in quite amazing ways, that should not be taken to mean that he does not continue to use the means he has given us to restore our health. There have been tragedies resulting from the idea that it is wrong, or lacking in faith somehow, to consult a doctor or take medication. At the same time, we all have to recognise the realities of life and death, because ultimately we do not choose to become alive, and neither can we avoid the fact that one day our earthly existence will cease, whether through accident, illness or old age.

The Christian faith asserts confidently that this life is not an end in itself, that something far greater and more wonderful awaits us beyond it. We look forward to eternal life as God's promise to all who believe in him, and look back to the resurrection of Jesus Christ as his demonstration and guarantee of that. This life makes sense only in the context of the life to come. Christian healing is therefore concerned with far more than our physical well-being or the issues of this life. An over-emphasis on the miraculous or spectacular will probably raise some people's expectations unhelpfully, but it can also trap us into wrong ideas about God and about our earthly existence. For the most part society has lost any concept of a future life, and consequently makes this one its primary focus. The philosophy that follows from this is that the longer it lasts the better it must be. In contrast, Christian healing is less concerned with extending our duration on this planet or making it a bit more comfortable than with enabling us to enter into a deeper relationship with our loving Father so that we become more whole as people, living now in the light of what is yet to be.

HEALING IN THE BIBLE

IT HAS TO BE SAID at the outset that the Bible was written in and for a very different culture from our own. The world in which we live contains much that Jesus' contemporaries would not have dreamt of, let alone believed possible. Indeed, the technological advances of the twentieth century would have amazed even our Victorian forbears. The Industrial Revolution changed the whole face of society, with a massive shift in the population from rural areas with an agriculture-based economy to large cities where the manufacturing processes were situated. But 200 years later another major change is taking place. The advent of the microprocessor and the advance of computer technology has led to massive reductions in the industrial workforce and as a result society's expectations and values have been reoriented again. Of course, much of this change has been beneficial. Cars are now routinely being fitted with catalytic converters to help prevent further pollution of the atmosphere; on average we're physically larger than our predecessors a century ago because of our improved diet and living conditions, and our life expectancy is substantially higher, for which we can thank developments in food technology; air travel may have a few drawbacks, but it is one of the safest forms of travel and has enabled many of the poorest and most deprived parts of the world to receive humanitarian and economic aid from more developed nations.

The trouble is, we have created for ourselves a host of problems, not least in the area of health. An example which I come across frequently is in the care of the elderly. Far more folk now live into their seventies and eighties than used to be the case, and while they are fit and healthy that is cause for rejoicing. But once infirmity and ill health set in, life can become a real trial. Formerly many of them would have died sooner because there would have been no medical aid to prolong their lives. Today we can keep our senior citizens alive for much longer, although the quality of their life may be very poor. A more acute illustration is that of the accident victim whose existence depends on a ventilator or artificial feeding. There have been court cases over this, and there is no simple answer, even for Christians – do we have a duty to prolong life to the maximum or should we accept the inevitability of death and allow the person to depart this life with dignity? There may be no straightforward solution to such moral dilemmas but the Christian healing ministry has to acknowledge and in some way respond to them. Humankind has used the necessity for such decisions as a way of 'standing in for God', and thus obviating any need to include him in its thinking. The Church has to come against this idea by demonstrating God's involvement in every part of our life, not least our health and welfare.

The Bible cannot directly address the issues raised by modern medical practice, but the concept of healing runs right through it. Inevitably we think first of Jesus' many recorded healing miracles, but he was in a tradition stretching back through Elijah and Elisha to Moses and even Abraham. Abraham did you ask? Well, he was not an agent of healing in quite the same way as Elijah or Jesus, but he is recorded as praying for the women in Abimelech's family to have the ability to bear children restored to them. This was in the context of forgiveness, a subject we shall return to again. In the Old Testament the word 'shalom' recurs many times and we usually translate it as 'peace'. For us peace often means an absence of something – noise, conflict or trouble. However in Hebrew it is a much wider concept, embracing everything to do with our wellbeing, not just physical health but also our relationships, contentment and salvation. 'Wholeness' is the best translation of 'shalom', a state which comes about 'when the will of God is being done, when there is a harmony of being at one with the purposes of the Creator' (Bishop Morris Maddocks). Sin destroys that oneness with our heavenly Father, because it runs counter to his will for us. The Prince of Peace was one of the titles Isaiah used to describe the Messiah (Isaiah 9:6), and by his incarnation, death and resurrection Jesus brings us forgiveness for our sins, thus restoring us to a right relationship with God our Father. That is the true meaning of peace, because only when we are at one with God and living according to his purposes can we begin to experience that true wholeness which transforms every part of our lives.

It is important to understand the links between sin, forgiveness and healing. Jesus himself was quite clear that not all illness or infirmity is the result of personal wrongdoing – if it were, we should all be ill the whole time! He specifically said of the young man whose sight he restored that his condition was not the result of his own or his parents' sin (John 9:2-3). However, we live in a fallen world, spoiled not just by the misdeeds of a few individuals but by the presence of evil; Paul expresses it in terms of 'fighting against the powers of this dark world, and against the spiritual forces of evil in the heavenly realms' (Ephesians 6:12). Sin affects all of us and lies within all of us. The tendency to go astray from God's will for us and to do our own thing is part of our fallen human nature and when we do, we cease to live in harmony with him, or with the rest of creation. Forgiveness is about the restoration of those relationships. The three Hebrew words used in the Old Testament to describe forgiveness illustrate this well. One conveys the idea of sin being covered over, so that it no longer comes between humankind and God; another brings in the concept of sin being carried away, of a barrier being removed; while the third indicates that the one who forgives bears no resentment or anger. The most frequently used word in the New Testament to indicate forgiveness also means 'to send away'. Forgiveness goes hand in hand with repentance, not a cringing admission of guilt but a complete change of mind and heart, as the Greek word *metanoia* implies. Jesus' preaching was always 'repent and believe the good news', and the early church, led by the apostles, followed his example (*cf* Mark 1:15/Acts 2:38).

The only condition for receiving forgiveness is that we ourselves are willing to forgive others on an unlimited basis, or as Jesus said on one occasion to Peter, 'not seven times but seventy times seven'. We cannot earn forgiveness from our heavenly Father under any circumstances. It is entirely a gift of his own free will and if we want to receive healing and become more whole we need only receive it from him into our lives.

Jesus' own name means 'Saviour' or 'Deliverer'. (It is the same as Joshua, who led the Israelites into the promised land.) The Greek word for 'salvation' is *soteria*, which can be translated equally as 'healing'. Interestingly, when William Tyndale translated the account of Zaccheus into English, he said 'today health has come to this house', whereas later translations have used the word 'salvation' instead. In Jesus' ministry healing was a sign of the coming and presence of God's kingdom, a demonstration of its power over all the forces of evil which spoil our lives and prevent us from being free to live as God intended us to. Theologians have debated at length whether that kingdom is a present or a future phenomenon. For the Jews God's present reign was over their nation, while his future reign would be over all nations. Jesus certainly taught that God's kingdom would at some future time include all peoples and things, but he wanted them to know also that by receiving him into their lives and following his ways, they could enter into that kingdom here and now and experience it as a reality in their own lives. In both word and deed, as Maddocks says, Jesus came to inaugurate the kingdom of God, not as a geographical entity but as his reign in people's hearts. When John the Baptist was in prison, he sent a message to Jesus asking whether he really was the promised Messiah. Jesus' response was to point to the evidence of his ministry – the deaf are made to hear, the blind can now see, the lame are dancing with joy . . . This is not the kingdom itself, but a sign of its reality both as a future hope and a present experience (see Matthew 11:2-6). Healing is part of the good news of God's kingdom, evidence that this is not just 'pie in the sky when we die', but something we can begin to enjoy here and now. Jesus' words and teachings are well enough known, but as we sometimes say, 'actions speak louder than words'. The miracles, (which is not really the most accurate translation of any of the New Testament words describing Jesus' supernatural acts) many of which involve people being made well from various illnesses and conditions, demonstrate that Jesus' words were not the empty ramblings of an eccentric or megalomaniac. On the contrary, he was so unpopular because the religious authorities recognised the power of God that lay behind what he said, as did the crowds, who claimed that no-one else spoke with such authority.

Interestingly, Jesus did not expect anyone to come to him in the Temple for a special ceremony before they could receive healing (though on one occasion he sent ten lepers to the Temple for the rite of cleansing – Luke 17:14). Instead he healed people wherever they were – in their homes, in the market-place, on their own, in small groups and in large crowds. That is not an argument against healing services, but it does indicate that when the Church is approached for the ministry of healing it must start where people are, and make no discrimination about who should receive it. Jesus certainly did not set out to make for himself a reputation as a great healer or miracle-worker. When King Herod asked him to perform a few miracles to establish his credentials, Jesus refused, although he could have saved his life by agreeing (Luke 23:8-9). He could doubtless have put on an act for the authorities had he so wished, but he knew that his Father had not sent him for that reason. 'I have come to do the will of him who sent me', John quotes him as saying (John 6:38). And it is John more than the other evangelists who emphasises the work that Jesus came to do, a work that was not complete until Calvary, when Jesus, hanging in agony on the Cross, cried 'It is finished!' (John 19:30). If he had wanted to be Jesus Christ Superstar there could have been no less effective way of achieving that aim than by submitting to death as a criminal after a cruelly unfair trial. Yet it is through Jesus' death we can be restored to a relationship with our heavenly Father and begin to experience the wholeness for which we were created. Not every sin causes an illness, of course, nor is all suffering the consequence of an individual's wrongdoing, as Jesus once pointed out to his disciples (John 9:1-3), but the way to wholeness and healing is through the cross, which as Paul says in his letter to the Ephesians, has broken down the dividing wall between humankind and God (2:14-18). And Peter, in his first letter to some early Christians, states clearly that it is by Jesus' wounds that we can be healed (1 Peter 2:24). God does not give mystical magic powers to a few favoured Christians. The power to extend the healing and wholeness available through Jesus' death is a gift of the Holy Spirit for the whole of Christ's body, the church. The New Testament writers do not recognise the gift of healing being exercised other than under the authority of the church; it is quite against the teaching of the Bible and the church for individuals to use this gift for self-promotion. We can exercise it in his name and for his glory only when we accept as he did the role of a servant. And in so doing our aim is never to draw attention to ourselves, nor to try and get around National Health Service waiting lists, but to bring reconciliation between God and those we minister to. As Paul says to the Christians at Corinth, the ministry of reconciliation has been entrusted to us (2 Corinthians 5:18).

So how was Christian healing ministered in the early church?. The driving force behind the first Christians was their knowledge that the crucified Jesus had indeed been raised from death by his Father, and was alive now and for evermore. All the sermons recorded in the book of Acts are centred on the resurrection, and for the New Testament writers the whole Christian faith stands or falls on it. Many scholars have used the different accounts in the gospels to try and argue that the bodily resurrection either did or did not take place, but however the accounts are interpreted, no-one can dispute that ever since then vast numbers of people down the centuries have claimed to experience personally the presence and power of the risen Christ in their lives. How else would it be possible to explain the continued existence of the church over two thousand years in the face of opposition, hardship and internal division? Why have so many Christians been willing to endure ill-treatment or even death for the sake of what they believe? Quite simply, they know he is alive in them, a belief based not on subjective feelings alone but on an objective reality. The resurrection was the ultimate demonstration of the power of God's kingdom, a power already seen in the signs and wonders performed by Jesus during his ministry, particularly in healing people from physical illness and raising them from death.

The first miracle recorded in the book of Acts was the healing of the crippled beggar who sat by the Temple gate scraping together a meagre existence from the generosity of the passers-by. Peter and John, on their way to Evening Prayer in the Temple, had no cash to throw into his bowl, but their belief in the power of the risen Christ was such that they had no hesitation in claiming his authority over the handicap. Having told the man to get up and start walking, Peter then took his hand and helped him to his feet, an act of faith if ever there was! A few moments later the man was jumping around praising God for his healing, much to the amazement of the onlookers and the disgust of the religious authorities. Peter explained to them that this man had been made whole by the power of the risen Christ, who only a few weeks previously had been put to death as a criminal. The reaction of the rulers and elders is an indication of how much they regarded this kind of activity as a threat (Acts 3 & 4). In fact, healing miracles seemed to be the norm for the earliest Christians, and they were evidently an unexceptionable part of everyday church life. Paul mentions healing as one of the gifts of the Holy Spirit (1 Corinthians 12:1-13) and by the time James wrote his epistle, there was a degree of formalisation in how it was exercised (James 5:16). Both of these passages emphasise that the Christian healing ministry can only exist as part of the activity of the whole body of Christ.

The biblical witness is clear. The power of God is able to heal people of all kinds of diseases and conditions. There can be little doubt that the New Testament writers expected this to be used along with all the other gifts of the Spirit as part of church life. The question then remains; is this relevant to our society at the end of the twentieth century? To answer it, we shall look first at what has happened over the intervening nineteen hundred years.

HEALING IN THE CHURCH

ALTHOUGH the Biblical evidence is relatively limited, because the writers of the New Testament do not overemphasise it as an activity in its own right, it seems clear that the gift of healing was exercised by the early church as a normal part of its ministry. In 1 Corinthians 12 Paul refers to 'gifts of healing' as one of the nine gifts of the Holy Spirit (though this is certainly not intended as an exhaustive or exclusive list). Living so close to the apostolic age, most first century Christians would have regarded healing miracles as signs of God's kingdom, his power at work in transforming the lives of all kinds of people. That did not come to an end immediately. In fact, the church combined the ministry of healing with the proclamation of the Good News for at least three centuries. Among the early church Fathers both Justin Martyr and Tertullian testify to individuals who had received healing in the name of Jesus. The great Bishop of Lyons, Irenaeus, witnessed to all manner of healings like those described in the New Testament, and even pointed out that heretics were unable to minister healing because they had no access to the power of God. Later on another Bishop, Cyprian of Carthage, warned that worldliness was creeping into the church, which in turn was robbing prayer of its power. This grew even more evident when the emperor Constantine was converted and Christianity became the accepted norm in society. The need to organise a system of belief and theology, partly to counter heresy, led to a decreasing awareness of God's power to save and heal. Among the great theological minds of the fourth and fifth centuries, men like Basil the Great and John Chrysostom all accepted that the church is commissioned to heal in the name of Jesus. But before long this became the exception. Martin of Tours, Francis of Assisi and some of the Celtic fathers were among those prepared to acknowledge this aspect of the church's ministry, but for the most part the church had forgotten what it had been called to do. However, since the Reformation there has been a steady increase in the number of reported healings, with a massive rise in the past two or three decades. Interestingly, the incidence of miracles seems to be connected with times of revival in religious life. One example of this was John Wesley, whose ministry among the poor and neglected led on occasion to unexpected and inexplicable healings, much to the disgust of the hierarchy of the established church.

So why has the twentieth century seen such a growth, not just in the number of reported healings, but also in the level of interest shown by the church and Christian people in the ministry of healing? Part of the answer lies in the insecurity of our age. For several centuries the thinking of the Enlightenment held sway in Western society. While this was by no means wholly bad, it led to the general view that everything could be explained rationally, and that humankind was gradually getting better. Two World Wars certainly dented this view of life, but more recently there has been a general awareness that we aren't really as clever as we thought. We have done massive damage to our environment in the interests of economic growth, more people are suffering from famine, poverty and warfare than ever before, and technological advances have left us with frightening moral dilemmas. We seem incapable of controlling the situations we have created. As a result there is a great sense of despair about the future, and a tendency to look away from the rational and tangible towards the inexplicable and mystical. The growth in the New Age movement (more of an umbrella term for many disparate groupings) and interest in supernatural phenomena demonstrates how much we need to find something to hold on to outside ourselves.

Inevitably, a few unscrupulous characters have latched on to this and used it for their own selfish gain. The bad press given to American 'televangelists' has raised doubts in the minds of many about the legitimacy of getting involved in this area. The current obsession with health and associated issues is by no means restricted to the Christian church, therefore. In fact, the church has taken a long time to recognise how important its role is in a society which is looking to all kinds of strange belief systems and religious or pseudo-religious groups for the answer to its insecurities and hang-ups. Of course we need to be careful to avoid any suggestion of being manipulative or self-seeking, but that is true of every aspect of the church's ministry. The need for exercising wisdom and discretion is hardly an argument against getting involved – after all, no-one has argued that because of the care we need to take when on the roads, we should avoid driving a car. In fact, the present confused and volatile situation is one the church is especially qualified to address, since it has the message of good news, of new life in Christ, and of healing in his name rather than under the dubious auspices of the plethora of religious groups existing today, or under the spurious authority of self-styled and self-appointed 'apostles'.

The Christian healing ministry has by no means been confined to the extreme fringes of the church. In the Church of England the Guild of Health was formed in 1904 by a well-known musician and Anglican layman Dr Percy Dearmer and others, while in the following year another Anglican layman, James Moore Hickson, formed the Society of Emmanuel (later to become the Divine Healing Mission). Hickson had a remarkable worldwide ministry with colleagues such as Prebendary Carlisle, who founded the Church Army after being healed of a back condition. Two centres for Christian healing were established at the Old Rectory at Crowhurst, always linked with the Divine Healing Mission, and at Burrswood in Kent, which was set up by Dorothy Kerin, a young woman healed miraculously on her deathbed. In 1944 Archbishop William Temple called together the Churches' Council for Health and Healing 'to educate Christian people . . . to provide knowledge of spiritual healing and fuller co-operation and understanding between doctors and clergy and all those engaged in health in the full sense'. More recently, the 1978 Lambeth Conference passed a resolution praising God for the renewal of this ministry in the church in recent times and affirming its belief in both healing the sick and proclaiming the good news. Not that this was restricted to the Anglican Church. Many other denominations became more committed to healing in the name of Christ, and churches across the world began to take seriously their commission to heal the sick as well as to go into the whole world and preach the gospel. More recently the charismatic renewal has profoundly influenced many churches, not least the Church of England, and its emphasis on the gifts of the Holy Spirit has led many to exercise a ministry of healing under the church's authority. Some are cautious about the whole renewal movement, but while there have been some excesses, the concept of every member ministry and belief in a sovereign God who can heal and save has been a source of spiritual growth and vitality. It is interesting to note that in parallel with the growth of the Christian healing ministry has come a corresponding growth in ecumenical activity. Healing services are just one example of the sort of joint venture which brings together Christians of many different traditions, from charismatic to catholic, from liberal to conservative, from evangelical to Pentecostal, healing the wounds of past division.

BODY, MIND AND SPIRIT: DIFFERENT KINDS OF HEALING

WE HAVE already established that Christian healing encompasses far more than just the improvement of our physical health. Indeed, many agencies of Christian healing will say that the largest proportion of their time and prayer is spent dealing with emotional and physical problems. Francis MacNutt was an American priest in the Dominican order who discovered that God had given him a striking ministry of healing the sick. A man of impeccable intellectual and spiritual credentials, he began to be involved in praying for healing in prayer groups and was soon recognised as the Roman Catholic Church's leading authority on this subject. In 1974 he wrote his book 'Healing', in which he described both his theology and his experiences of prayer for healing. It is still one of the best selling books on this whole subject. In it he outlines three basic kinds of healing which may be needed, and goes on to detail the kind of prayer required in each case.

i   Physical sickness or injury, caused by illness or accident. Clearly there is a wide range of severity, from a mild bout of 'flu through to a terminal condition, or from a cut knee to a broken back. In general terms the cause of these is fairly obvious, and not attributable to personal sin – we all catch a cold from time to time, or need antibiotics when we pick up an infection through being run down or tired.

ii   Emotional sickness and pain, rooted either in distressing personal circumstances in the present or in damage and hurt from the past (frequently from childhood). This has come to the fore greatly in the last few years, even in secular counselling, and mental states such as anxiety may well result in bodily pain or discomfort, a fact now recognised far beyond the confines of the Christian church.

iii Spiritual sickness, which MacNutt identifies as the consequence of personal sin. This obviously applies primarily to those who accept the Christian faith and ethical code, but it is vital to distinguish between this and unhelpful guilt feelings. Some people become over-concerned in an unhealthy way with their own wrongdoing, whether or not they are morally in the wrong. These very strong feelings of guilt can cause terrible damage to both spiritual and emotional health, and should be discouraged since they are certainly not God-given. We have our consciences to prick us when we start to deviate from God's ways, but the Christian faith teaches quite clearly that in Christ God forgives all our sins and puts them behind us. Forgiveness leads to freedom from the bondage of guilt, which makes a great deal of sense of the practice of confession, both corporate and private.

This leads to the first of the four kinds of prayer identified by MacNutt, the prayer of, and perhaps for, repentance. In confessing our sin aloud we are opening ourselves to receive God's forgiveness and can then put behind us both the sin and its consequences because God has dealt with them in the death and resurrection of Jesus Christ. Those engaged in a specific ministry of healing may find themselves hearing confessions and praying with someone for repentance. It cannot be stressed enough that this should be done entirely without judgment, manipulation or condemnation. Healing will come through the assurance of sins forgiven. The second prayer is for inner or emotional healing, which from personal experience is the most frequently used form. The person concerned may well release confidential or personal information about their life while this is happening, and again they should never feel condemned or in any way inferior. The third type of prayer is for physical healing of one kind or another. However, these are all interchangeable, since God created us whole, and it is not possible to isolate just one area. As a simple example, think how a cold or viral infection can lay us low and make us feel depressed and spiritually down. As often as not these areas are interlinked and prayer for one of them may well have an impact elsewhere. The fourth prayer is that used for deliverance from evil spirits or demonic forces, which may be evident in any of the three aspects mentioned by MacNutt. Many Christian ministers will testify to the power that evil can have over an individual, although it has to be said that this is not the norm. While some kind of oppression or possession by demonic forces may be the root cause of the problem being presented, this should never be automatically assumed. Some sensitive souls have been terribly hurt by an over zealous minister 'accusing' them of being possessed by an evil spirit when their real need was inner healing. It should be a 'last resort diagnosis', and dealt with by those who have a recognised ministry in this area. Dealing with the forces of evil is a matter to be taken seriously, and handled with great care and sensitivity. In general it would be inappropriate to do this in a healing service.

There is a wide overlap between this kind of prayer and counselling. A problem is presented and listened to, a response may well be made and something is done to face up to the issue in question at least, if not to ease the burden. The problem with this in a liturgical context is primarily one of time. For the most part the service itself is long enough only to pray briefly with those who request it, any extended prayer and ministry being left until afterwards. Nor will everyone present want specific prayer, in which case they could be left in their seats for an uncomfortably long time while others are coming to be prayed for. Having said this, there is a strong possibility that if the congregation is invited to say what their prayer request is, those ministering will hear a wide variety of problems, pains and suffering, even from a relatively small group. I well remember leading a service for some Christian leaders in Germany which was designed primarily to demonstrate how to organise and conduct healing in a liturgical context. When I asked those who so wished to come forward to the altar rail and indicate what they would like prayer for, I was confronted with a stream of people, all with real and deep needs – a woman whose daughter had committed suicide; a young mother of two whose husband was dying of cancer; a father with a son who was disabled and very demanding. There was even a confession of marital infidelity! As you might imagine, this was a time-consuming and exhausting process which left the two ministers completely drained. At the same time it was a profoundly moving experience which somehow touched even those who did not receive specific prayer. As MacNutt points out, it is essential to be sensitive to the needs of each individual without losing sight of the whole act of worship.

At this point we must be clear that such healing prayer, important as it undoubtedly is, is not a better and quicker alternative to the medical profession. God has created the natural healing processes in us, and he normally activates them through the work of doctors and surgeons, psychiatrists and counsellors, nurses and paramedics. Some Christian ministers of healing have set up a false boundary between prayer and medicine, as though God can only work through the former, and implying that using the latter is a sign that faith is seriously lacking. This can only be described as at best a poor theology of creation and at worst potentially dangerous. I heard of someone a few years ago who contracted cancer at a relatively young age. He was convinced by other Christians that medical treatment was not an option because God would heal him as a result of prayer. He failed to go to a doctor until it was far too late and he died, leaving a young family behind. Not surprisingly his widow has barely entered a church since. How much pain and suffering was caused by this well-intentioned 'advice' can only be imagined. Maybe he would not have lived in any case, but no-one had the chance to find out. As a result I always now ensure that I give some indication of what might happen as a result of prayer for healing, because false expectations can be very damaging. By no means everyone will receive immediate bodily healing, despite the claims of some evangelists, and inner healing may well take place over an extended period as different anxieties and issues come to the surface. It is a cruel deception to allow people to think that healing is automatic if you pray in the right way, and to give counsel to the effect that doctors are unnecessary could be disastrous. Far better for doctors and ministers to work together as a team so that healing can take place.

Given that within a normal service there will be very little time for individual prayer, how should those ministering pray for those who approach them? If forgiveness is sought or required, a suitable prayer can be read aloud or extemporised dealing as necessary with the sin in question. MacNutt also says that many people find it difficult to receive forgiveness because they will not forgive others. Jesus several times highlighted this to his followers, not least in teaching them the Lord's Prayer – 'Forgive us our sins, as we forgive those who sin against us'. We receive forgiveness in the measure that we are prepared to give it ourselves. We all sin regularly in many and various ways, but the sin of 'unforgiveness' is the one most likely to hinder our healing. Within the Anglican tradition corporate confession is the norm at all services, although there are differing views on the practice of private confession. To hear the words of assurance that our sins are permanently forgiven by God can release his healing power in our lives and replace the 'chains' of guilt and guilty feelings with his love. A healing service without an act of confession by the whole congregation would be missing one of its most important dimensions. While individual confession may best be conducted privately, not only for reasons of confidentiality but also to restrict the time taken up, it is also an essential part of the Christian healing ministry.

To pray for physical healing is likewise a relatively straightforward procedure. It requires only that we listen to the person who approaches us with an illness or condition of some sort and then offer their situation in prayer to God. Or is it quite so easy? Of course we should listen to the problem as presented, but as all experienced Christian healing ministers will say, we have to listen equally to God's voice, which will often give us insights through the Holy Spirit into the specific things for which we should pray. This may sometimes seem like nothing more than intuition, but after a while we recognise when God is giving us an understanding of what is being said which will enable us to pray in a more focused and helpful way. The other requirements are discernment and courage. Discernment is not just a natural capacity for seeing beneath the surface. It is a God-given spiritual gift which in the context of Christian healing helps us to identify when we should pray and for whom, as well as how. It would not be possible to minister to every single need, so it is important to recognise the right time to pray with and for a particular person. A lack of discernment could lead to much time and effort being misdirected, and quite possibly to the whole idea of Christian healing being misunderstood. Courage is also necessary, particularly at the start of such a ministry. It is not just a question of taking a deep breath and diving in – we can be courageous and bold in praying for healing because we are confident that God has given us that person to minister to at this time. Our confidence is in the Lord who heals, and as we obey his command to heal the sick we trust the results of that to him. We need to be very clear, however, that we are not promising or guaranteeing a full or even partial cure. False expectations, once aroused, usually lead to disenchantment and sometimes to a rejection of prayer for healing. As an example of this, we can see Peter and John outside the Temple, making their way to evening prayer and being accosted as they did so by a man born lame. All he wanted was money – what he received was a whole new life! We do not see the two disciples promising everyone such healing, but they knew they had to minister to this man. It must have taken a great deal of confidence and courage on their part to take his hand, lift him to his feet, and command him to walk in the name of Jesus.

Prayer for healing of a physical nature is frequently associated with other healing needs, especially in the area of emotions. Inner or emotional healing, as MacNutt says, lies somewhere between spiritual healing through confession and a bodily cure. The failings which might be put down to sin may be the consequence of events in the past, and what is needed in these cases is what Agnes Sanford, a great pioneer of Christian healing, described as 'healing of the memories'. This applies to all of us in some measure. No human being who has ever lived has gone through life without some anxieties and hang-ups coming from past bad experiences. However, when this becomes too distressing, or results in symptoms such as depression or some kind of compulsive, obsessive or addictive behaviour, prayer becomes an important element in their healing. This is an area where even now doctors feel they are on uncertain ground, because there is a severe limit to how much they can do for such symptoms. Damage from the past can fill people with fears and anxieties which profoundly affect their behaviour in certain respects. Prayer for this aspect of healing has two specific functions: to bring to the surface those events or traumas which are subconsciously conditioning our behaviour, and to ask God to deal with them so that they no longer do so. Clearly this might be a long process which could not reasonably take place within the restricted confines of a healing service, but it could nevertheless be started there. In the words of St Augustine's famous prayer, 'Our hearts are restless till they find their rest in you'. Prayer for inner healing is specifically directed towards enabling those in need to begin to find rest and peace in God which will calm their troubled state and bring them into greater wholeness of mind and spirit.

The last few years have seen a great increase of interest in the deliverance aspect of the Christian healing ministry. It is not something separate from the other parts of that ministry, but is another area to be borne in mind, and one that requires careful and sensitive handling. Regrettably it has attracted to itself some extreme views, not all of which have a close relationship with the Bible, Christian tradition or reason, and as a result some individuals have been left badly damaged by dangerous practices or misplaced zeal. One extreme is the standard twentieth century view that there is no such thing as an evil spirit or any other kind of agency by which the forces of evil can affect us. This argument is based on the relatively primitive attitudes of Jesus' day which we are told we no longer need to hold, because 'we know better'. Admittedly there are occasions in the Gospels when a condition described as 'an evil spirit' appears from our current medical knowledge to have a less sinister explanation (e. g. epilepsy). However, we cannot automatically assume from the very limited descriptions that this is the case, and in any event the reality of evil is evident all around and not disproved by one possible explanation. It would be unwise and untrue to the Christian faith to deny that there are times when an individual may need to be delivered from some kind of evil influence which is affecting his or her life and behaviour. The opposite extreme is to see evil spirits lurking behind every door and attribute to them all kinds of behaviour or attitude which may well have a much more mundane origin. The harm which can be caused by such an approach should not be under-estimated. Before anyone is told that they are possessed or oppressed in some way by an evil spirit, all other possibilities should be ruled out and there should be clear evidence that this is a correct diagnosis of the problem. There are four possible areas to consider, although it must be remembered that these may well be present in those whose need is for psychiatric treatment.

i   An awareness of the power of evil in the person receiving ministry. Some people who are genuinely oppressed in this way are conscious that they are somehow influenced by evil though we should beware of those who use such statements as an attention-seeking device or because they are very suggestible and naive.

ii   Prayer for physical, spiritual or inner healing which 'hasn't worked' (i. e. has had no discernible effect). All prayer has some effect, but it may be that beyond a certain level it is being blocked by a barrier of evil.

iii There is an element of obsessiveness and compulsion about the individual's behaviour in certain areas. Alcoholism, substance abuse and addiction, sexual perversion and a tendency to self-destruction may all indicate a need for the ministry of deliverance. Having said that, it is clear that not every member of Alcoholics Anonymous falls into this category, nor yet everyone drawn to abnormal sexual activity or drug abuse. Spiritual discernment is a prerequisite if those who come for ministry are to be prayed for properly and sensitively.

iv   There are behavioural manifestations that are so abnormal that we cannot find any explanation at a human level. These can be horrible and disturbing and should not be dealt with by anyone with little or no experience in this area.

As a general rule, it is best that deliverance is undertaken in private by an experienced team. It may well be the case that one or more ministers become aware of this kind of problem during a service but it should be deferred until later, to avoid causing distress or disturbance to other worshippers, and to ensure that the individual receives as much attention and time as necessary.

I am not happy with the idea of 'mass deliverance' which is sometimes practised at conferences and other large scale events. Jesus certainly did not use this approach, preferring instead to minister one-to-one. Nor is deliverance in a public arena something advocated in the Bible. Much better to tackle it in private where there is less risk of embarrassment or misinterpretation of what is going on.

How then should we pray for healing, and can anyone do it?

On a basic level all Christians can and should bring before God in their prayers those who are sick or in need. However, Paul states clearly that some Christians are given 'gifts of healing' (1 Corinthians 12:9) which suggests they have a specific task and ministry in that area. It is a gift which should be confirmed by the church fellowship too, as those who exercise it need to have the respect of the whole body of Christ. Everyone has to start somewhere, and there is no better way to learn than to minister with someone who already has experience of praying for the sick. There are no special techniques or tricks of the trade, nor is a postgraduate theology degree necessary. Sensitivity, discernment and a willingness to listen are the primary requirements, together with an openness to follow God's leading and pray according to that. Strong or extreme views may be a hindrance for some people, and those who hold them could deter others from seeking ministry as a result. Ideally each church should have a team of respected and sensitive members who are able and willing to exercise a God-given ministry of Christian healing to the whole fellowship and community without causing controversy, division or unhappiness. There should be no hint of status being attached to this (nor yet to any other form of Christian service) as it could easily become a vehicle for those who seek power and influence. How should they go about it? That is covered in the next couple of sections.

THE LAYING ON OF HANDS
AND ANOINTING WITH OIL

PERHAPS the most familiar characteristic of the Christian healing ministry is the practice of the minister laying hands on the head of the person who has come for prayer. This may seem rather odd to the uninitiated but it is worth understanding and explaining this action to avoid any suspicions or misinterpretation. Throughout the Bible it is recognised as a symbol of an individual receiving God's power, often for a specific task. In the early church those who were set apart for such a ministry received the laying on of hands from the apostles as a sort of commissioning for their future work (Acts 6:6/ 1 Timothy 4:14). As far as healing is concerned Jesus frequently touched people who were sick as part of their healing process, particularly those who were disregarded by everyone else or avoided because they were deemed unclean (cf Matthew 14:31/Mark 8:23 etc). Touch is no less important a sense than the other four, and its use as part of the healing ministry reflects that. It conveys to us the idea of a physical reality and a feeling of immediacy. Intimacy is also implied by touch. The idea of the minister laying hands on the person coming for prayer is to bring to them an awareness of the power of God coming upon them, of the reality of his presence and work in their lives and of his personal involvement with them in their circumstances. Even for those who are not sick the laying on of hands can convey a blessing – in fact this is the most frequent use of the rite in Scripture.

However, we need to be quite clear that those who are recognised as having this spiritual gift do not possess weird magical powers, nor are they super-sensitive spiritually. There is no hint of any 'supernatural' power being granted to a select few. We are all given the gifts of the Holy Spirit for the benefit of the whole body of Christ, and there is no status difference between any of them. Strange manifestations such as tingling in the fingers or a sensation of warmth may well be the experience of those engaging in the laying on of hands, but as John Richards points out candidly in his excellent book *The Question of Healing Services*, such physical phenomena are no more spiritual than hiccoughs! We are told on one occasion that Jesus was aware of power going out of him (the woman who touched the edge of his coat was responsible for this) but otherwise the Bible does not mention physical sensations. The emphasis is always on God's grace and activity in bringing healing, not on anything done by the minister. Interestingly, Jesus is never recorded as touching demoniacs when delivering them from evil spirits.

The laying on of hands when exercised in a service needs to be handled sensitively and with great care. Many people are unused to the idea of such an act even finding a place in the liturgy, and if it is performed in an aggressive or cavalier way they are not likely to pay a return visit.

It is also vital to ensure that there are no misunderstandings about what is happening when the minister lays hands on someone's head or shoulder. The 'New Age' movement is nothing very new, and every generation has had some kind of belief in invisible forces which can heal us through psychic power. Christian healing is not about the transfer of spiritual energy via someone's fingertips, regardless of physical sensation when engaging in prayer with the laying on of hands. Even when the woman with a haemorrhage touched Jesus' coat and he experienced a 'power loss', he was quite clear that his clothing did not have magical properties – the woman's healing was the result of her faith in him (Luke 8:48). The fact that someone has been inexplicably healed or cured does not necessarily mean that this is a spiritual phenomenon; even if it is 'spiritual', it would be very unwise to assume that this is of the Holy Spirit. Indeed, many evil or satanic groups claim 'healings' as part of their repertoire, though it would be instructive to know the durability or extent of these.

Then there is the question of expectations. It would be cruel to allow those who are seriously ill or troubled in some way to believe that receiving the touch of a minister automatically guarantees a physical improvement or pain reduction. John Richards suggests helpfully that the laying on of hands is best regarded as a 'blessing of the sick' which will certainly bestow some divine benefit, but not necessarily in a physical form. The congregation need to be fully aware that Christian healing embraces far more than the removal of a bodily problem. Encouraging them to receive ministry for emotional and spiritual issues as well as illnesses will keep their vision of the healing ministry in a broad perspective and focus their expectations away from medical conditions.

Oil was a basic element of living in Israel, but it was also used for anointing kings and priests and certain liturgical items. Jesus was the Messiah, the 'anointed one', and the title 'Christ' is the Greek translation of that. Christians are described as those 'anointed' with the Holy Spirit. Not surprisingly the early church took over the symbolism of oil and seems to have used it extensively. James 5:13-16 indicates that the use of oil with prayer for the sick was a normal practice among the early Christians. Quite wrongly it has been viewed by some as an exclusively Catholic rite but this is not so. Increasingly it is being used by Christians of all denominations as part of the healing ministry, and while perhaps its administration should be sparing in order to retain its significance, no-one needs to be afraid of it as part of the liturgy, and suggestions for its incorporation are included later in this book.

THE HEALING SERVICE

T HE COMMENT 'Every service should be a healing service' is
frequently made when the question arises of a service
specifically based on Christian healing. In one sense it is quite
true. Every service should be a healing experience in that it
brings worshippers closer to the risen Christ whose very
presence makes us whole. However, that does not really tackle
the issue – in fact it could be used to try and escape from our
God-given commission to heal the sick. The question of how
to plan and conduct a service which is dedicated to celebrating
and ministering the healing power of Christ cannot be dealt
with by referring to the spiritual temperature of other services.
It could be argued that healing services are nowhere
advocated in the Bible; again this is true, but Christmas carol
services are not mentioned either. Whether in one-to-one
ministry or counselling, or in a liturgical setting, we are
commanded by God to preach the good news of his kingdom
and to heal the sick as a sign of its power and goodness.

The underlying assumption is that during the service the
ministry of prayer for healing with the laying on of hands will be
prominent. It can be included at different points, and
administered in a variety of ways, but the objective of a healing
service is to focus on this as the means by which God's healing
power is released in the lives of those who have requested
prayer for a particular problem, be this physical, emotional or
spiritual. There are a number of basic questions which need to
be answered before the exact format of the liturgy can be
determined, but whatever shape the service takes, the ministry
of healing will be one of the focal points, if not the primary one.

Is the service to be ecumenical?
There are many good reasons for joining in with other local
churches and traditions for a healing service, not least the
symbolic healing of the rifts which have previously existed

between different branches of the Christian church. It provides a great opportunity for members of those churches to work together in the same cause, both in planning a service and in conducting it. As a result, all can learn from each other's perspectives and approaches and a greater sense of unity and purpose is engendered. The main disadvantage of an ecumenical healing service is that it is unlikely to be Eucharistic. The differences between the various denominations on this issue are such that it would probably be counter-productive to try and reach agreement, and even if an acceptable structure were to be achieved some would prefer to 'opt out'. The other potential disadvantage is the factor of the 'lowest common denominator'. The concern to be seen co-operating and working together can sometimes result in a blandness which may cause offence to no one, but brings no benefit either. Each church can make its own distinctive contribution, through readings, prayers, sermons and other elements, and the differences can be used positively. If these are all ironed out the overall 'feel' will be very flat.

Is the service to be Eucharistic?
There are many who believe that a healing service without the Eucharist is not really complete. Our healing comes from the crucified and risen Lord whom we celebrate in the bread and wine, and in receiving those elements we also share in his eternal life. He touches our lives and makes them whole as we open ourselves to him. In the New Testament, as we have already seen, the Greek word *sozo* means both to heal and to save. The sacrament which celebrates our salvation can also therefore bring God's healing power. Theologically it makes sense to link healing with the Eucharist. There is also a practical advantage in that many folk will already be familiar with this form of service, and what may be an unfamiliar ministry is placed in a well-known context. The obvious difficulties are that ecumenical co-operation may well not be possible, and that not only does the Eucharist take longer but it has a natural climax which may be felt to detract from the

ministry of healing. The latter point can be addressed by good planning and preparation, but a decision will have to be taken in principle as to whether or not the service should be Eucharistic. To a large degree this will depend on the tradition of the church and its general approach, though it has to be noted that a majority of churches do opt to include the ministry of healing in this setting, regardless of churchmanship.

Should the service be formal or more informal?
Again, there is no 'right' answer. Formality has in its favour a sense of security which may be important to those who are afraid things might get 'out of hand'. It creates a framework which can contain any emotional excesses and which enables everyone to see where the service is going. Unfortunately it can also become very stiff and starchy, just another ritual for the church to indulge itself with, rather than the means by which the healing power of Christ touches people's lives at the point of their deepest need. Informality can give a great sense of freedom and provides a more relaxed environment for those who are very likely to have come feeling tense and anxious. It can, however, trivialise the ministry of healing if not handled with care, and when taken to excess might frighten some who are not certain about what might happen next. Informality of approach should on no account be taken to imply that less planning and preparation are needed. Sloppiness and carelessness are unlikely to make anyone feel at ease, and may well deter some from opening themselves to God in such a sensitive setting.

Who should take part in the ministry of prayer with laying on of hands?
Many churches have agonised over this question, and many clergy have no doubt had to soothe ruffled feelings as a result! Paul is quite clear in his first letter to the church at Corinth that the Holy Spirit gives to God's people gifts of healing, among many others. Not all will have this particular

gift, and those who do must exercise it only in the context of the whole body of Christ. Regrettably, there are some who will be attracted to the ministry of healing for the wrong reasons. They may see some kind of spiritual glamour attached to it, for example, or use it as a way to exert power over others. It is not always easy to identify such motives immediately, but they are inherently destructive and will very rapidly give people wrong ideas about the Christian healing ministry. Others may feel it will put them on a higher plane spiritually, or draw them closer to God in a way not possible through other forms of ministry. The motivation in this case may be commendable, but there's no Biblical justification for the notion that God somehow rates this ministry as superior to more mundane tasks in his kingdom. Indeed, if those who engage in it are perceived as 'holier than thou', or spiritually out of reach of mere mortals, they will also succeed in putting others off.

The most important consideration for this, as for every other ministry, is that the person exercising it not only feels God has called and equipped them for it, but is also recognised as such by the rest of the fellowship. If no-one identifies the gift of healing in an individual it is unlikely that that person or the ministry entrusted to them will be taken seriously. There is no particularly suitable personality type, and neither is it necessary for the minister to be ordained or even trained, though this latter has obvious benefits. Apart from having a recognised and identifiable gift in this area and a calling from God to engage in this ministry, those who take part in a healing service should be sensitive and non-judgemental listeners and open to the Spirit's work in their own lives. Indeed, those who have received healing themselves often prove to be the most effective ministers. They should also be willing to work in pairs and as part of a team. God wants us to work together, and ministering in partnership with someone else not only provides more insights and greater balance in approach but also prevents us from becoming too self-regarding. It gives a sense of support and unity, too, as different temperaments and backgrounds combine to bring God's healing power to the suffering. The best training for ministering healing in the name of Christ is to do it with someone experienced, though it may also be helpful for a whole team to attend a conference or seminar occasionally, to broaden its understanding and knowledge and receive theological input and practical help. While this may not be absolutely necessary, it is nonetheless desirable if at all possible. A willingness to learn and grow is a notable characteristic of an effective minister.

How should the healing service be organised?

The rest of this book contains a variety of liturgical ideas for a Christian healing service, be it Eucharistic, ecumenical, charismatic or catholic. Often the structure of the service will be immediately apparent. An Anglican Eucharist, for example, will have a recognisable shape, regardless of any alternative material included, and at whatever point the ministry of laying on of hands takes place. If the sacrament is not to be part of the service then the time of ministry would normally come towards the end, after the Ministry of the Word. There are a number of different views about how to handle the time of ministry. Some prefer to ask members of the congregation to come up, kneel or sit at a suitable spot, and explain their prayer needs. Others invite those who wish to come forward to do so, but not to say anything other than their name. If the service is Eucharistic, it may be logical to invite people to come up for prayer after they have received Communion, or even to remain at the altar rail (although this could cause confusion to those still waiting to receive the bread and wine). My own church asks that everyone remain at the altar-rail to receive a short blessing, which has the added advantage that everyone receives the laying on of hands and no-one needs therefore to feel embarrassed or self-conscious about coming forward. I have not yet encountered anyone who finds this difficult or objects to it. There is no one correct solution and the approach adopted will depend in part on the church's architecture, tradition and setting.

Some example services are laid out at the end of the book, and there are also a number of suggestions for words which might be appropriate to accompany the ministry of healing. These can be used and adapted to fit any local situation. Seasonal material is also incorporated – there is no reason to abandon the healing ministry just because it is Christmas or Easter!

PRAYERS

INTRODUCTORY AND CONCLUDING SENTENCES

INTRODUCTORY and concluding sentences are not compulsory, but often help to establish a particular theme or season, to start the service off or to sum it up. They can be drawn from one of the chosen readings or from elsewhere in the Bible. It is also possible to include a congregational response as a spoken word of praise or call to worship. The following selection covers a variety of seasons and themes.

ADVENT

Minister	The glory of the Lord will be revealed and all people together will see it. (Isaiah 40:5)
All	Jesus, our coming king, we praise and adore you.
Minister	The true light that gives light to all people is coming into the world. (John 1:9)
All	Jesus, Light of the world, we praise and adore you.
Minister	The light will break forth like the dawn; our healing will quickly appear. (Isaiah 58:8)
All	Jesus, Saviour and healer, we praise and adore you.

John the Baptist said, 'I have seen and I testify
that this is the Son of God'. (John 1:34)

The angel said to Mary,
'Nothing is impossible with God' (Luke 1:37)
'Peace, peace to those far and near', says the Lord.
'and I will heal them.' (Isaiah 57:19)

Jeremiah said, 'Heal me, Lord, and I shall be healed;
save me and I shall be saved'. (Jeremiah 17:14)

CHRISTMAS

Minister   The Sun of Righteousness is risen
with healing in his wings. (Malachi 4:2)

All   Jesus, our newborn king,
we worship and adore you.

Minister   The rising sun will come to us from heaven,
to shine on those living in darkness
and to guide our feet into the path of peace.
(Luke 1:79)

All   Jesus, Son of the Most High,
we worship and adore you.

Minister   He will be called Wonderful Counsellor,
Mighty God,
Everlasting Father,
Prince of Peace. (Isaiah 9:6)

All   Jesus, our Immanuel,
we worship and adore you.

The grace of God that brings healing has appeared to all.
(Titus 2:11)

Shout aloud and sing for joy, O people of Zion,
for great is the Holy One of Israel among you. (Isaiah 12:6)

Arise, shine, for your light has come
and the glory of the Lord rises upon you. (Isaiah 60:1)

EPIPHANY

Minister	The Lord says, 'My name will be great among the nations, from the rising to the setting of the sun.' (Malachi 1:11)
All	Jesus, king of the nations, we praise your holy name.
Minister	A voice came from heaven, saying, 'You are my Son, whom I love; with you I am well pleased'. (Mark 1:11)
All	Jesus, Word become flesh, we praise your holy name.
Minister	We have seen his glory, the glory of the one and only Son, who came from the Father, full of grace and truth'. (John 1:14)
All	Jesus, true God and true humanity, we praise your holy name.

Simeon said,
'My eyes have seen your salvation,
which you have prepared in the sight of all people.' (Luke 2:31)

The Magi bowed down and worshipped Jesus,
opened their treasures and presented him with
gifts of gold and frankincense and myrrh. (Luke 2:11)

Nations will see your righteousness and all kings your glory;
you will be called by a new name that the mouth of the Lord
will bestow. (Isaiah 62:2)

LENT

Minister   O Lord my God,
I called to you for help and you healed me.
(Psalm 30:2)

All   Sing to the Lord and praise his holy name.

Minister   The sacrifice of God is a broken spirit;
a broken and contrite heart, O God,
you will not despise. (Psalm 51:17)

All   Create in us clean hearts, O God.

Minister: The compassions of the Lord never fail.
They are new every morning.

All: The Lord is our portion;
we will wait for him. (Lamentations 3:22-24)

The lost son said,
'I have sinned against heaven and before you.
I am no longer worthy to be called your son.' (Luke 15:21)

The tax collector would not even look up to heaven but said,
'God, have mercy on me, a sinner.' (Luke 18:13)

The Lord said, 'I will heal my people
and will let them enjoy abundant peace and security.'
(Jeremiah 33:6)

PASSIONTIDE

Minister   Jesus himself bore our sins in his body on the tree,
so that we might die to sin and
live for righteousness.

All   By his wounds we have been healed. (1 Peter 2:24)

Minister   The punishment that brought us peace was upon
him.

All   By his wounds we have been healed. (Isaiah 53:5)

Minister   The Lord has torn us to pieces, but he will heal us.
He has injured us, but he will bind up our wounds.

All   Come, let us return to the Lord. (Hosea 6:1)

Jesus made himself nothing,
taking the very nature of a servant,
and became obedient to death
– even death on a cross. (Philippians 2:7 & 8)

This is love;
not that we loved God
but that he loved us
and sent his Son
as an atoning sacrifice for our sins. (1 John 4:10)

Jesus said,
Now is the Son of Man glorified,
and God is glorified in him.' (John 13:31)

EASTER

Minister   The death Jesus died, he died to sin, once and for all;
but the life he lives, he lives to God.

All   We are dead to sin but alive to God in Christ Jesus.
(Romans 6:10 & 11)

Minister   The one who raised the Lord Jesus from the dead
will also raise us with Jesus. (2 Corinthians 4:14)

All   We are dead to sin but alive to God in Christ Jesus.

Minister   Jesus said: 'I am the resurrection and the life.
All who believe in me will live,
even though they die;
and whoever lives and believes in me will never die.'

All   Yes Lord, we believe that you are the Christ,
the Son of God, who has come into the world.
(John 11:25-27)

Since death came through a man,
the resurrection of the dead comes also through a man.
(1 Corinthians 15:21)

Jesus came and stood among the disciples and said,
'Peace be with you.
As the Father has sent me,
I am sending you.' (John 20:19 & 21)

Jesus Christ is the faithful witness,
the firstborn from the dead,
and the ruler of the kings of the earth. (Revelation 1:5)

ASCENSIONTIDE

Minister   We have a great high priest who has gone through
the heavens,
Jesus the Son of God. (Hebrews 4:14)

All   You are worthy, our Lord and God,
to receive glory and honour and power.

Minister   Therefore God exalted Jesus to the highest place
and gave him the name that is above every name,
that at the name of Jesus every knee should bow.
(Philippians 2:9 & 10)

All   You are worthy, our Lord and God,
to receive glory and honour and power.

Minister   God raised Jesus from the dead
and seated him at his right hand in the heavenly
realms. (Ephesians 1:20)

All   You are worthy, our Lord and God,
to receive glory and honour and power.

We see Jesus, who was made a little lower than the angels,
now crowned with glory and honour because he suffered death.
(Hebrews 2:9)

We give thanks to you, Lord God Almighty,
who is and who was, and who is to come,
because you have taken your great power
and have begun to reign. (Revelation 11:17)

Christ is before all things,
and in him all things hold together. (Colossians 1:17)

PENTECOST

Minister The Lord says,
'I will pour out my Spirit on all people . . .
and everyone who calls on the name of the Lord
will be saved.' (Joel 2:28 & 32)

All We live in him and he in us,
because he has given us his Spirit.

Minister When the Spirit of truth comes,
he will guide you into all truth. (John 16:13)

All We live in him and he in us,
because he has given us his Spirit.

Minister To one is given through the Spirit the message of
wisdom,
to another the message of knowledge . . .
to another gifts of healing by that one Spirit.
(1 Corinthians 12:8 & 9)

All We live in him and he in us,
because he has given us his Spirit.

Peter said, 'It is Jesus' name and the faith that comes through him that has given this complete healing.' (Acts 3:16)

Jesus said, 'The Holy Spirit, whom the Father will send in my name, will teach you all things.' (John 14:26)

Jesus said, 'Go in peace; your faith has healed you.' (Luke 7:50)

GENERAL

Minister	Praise the Lord, O my soul, and forget not all his benefits.
All	He forgives all our sins and heals all our diseases. (Psalm 103:3)
Minister	I will exalt you, O Lord, for you lifted me out of the depths.
All	I called to you for help and you healed me. (Psalm 30:2)
Minister	The Lord heals the broken-hearted and binds up their wounds.
All	Great is our Lord and mighty in power. (Psalm 147:3,5)

The Lord says, 'I will heal their waywardness and love them freely.' (Hosea 14:4)

Jesus says, 'Come to me, all you who are weary and burdened, and I will give you rest.' (Matthew 11:28)

James says, 'Pray for each other so that you may be healed.' (James 5:16)

CONFESSIONS

CONFESSION is one of the most basic elements of our relationship with God. While it would be quite mistaken, as we have already established, to think that all illness or distress is the result of personal sin, we do what we know to be wrong very frequently. When we come to God confessing our wrongdoing, be it in thought, word or deed, it puts us right with him once again and makes us whole. Confession is therefore inextricably linked with healing. To make one's confession individually is an act which can have a powerful healing effect, but it cannot be part of a healing service. If this is requested by someone who has come forward for prayer, another suitable time and place should be arranged when time is not pressing and there is opportunity for further counsel.

The following selection of corporate confessions covers a variety of seasons and themes. Some are in the form of responses, others based on the Kyries. A number of absolutions are also included, which can be used with any of the confessions.

ADVENT

Lord Jesus, Light of the world,
you reveal the darkness of our sin and failure
and show us our need of your saving grace.

In your mercy,
forgive us and save us.

Lord Jesus, eternal Word,
you bring us the message of pardon and peace
and speak to us of your healing power.

In your mercy,
forgive us and save us.

Lord Jesus, coming king,
you promise us a place in your eternal kingdom
and fill our hearts with joy and hope.

In your mercy,
forgive us and restore us,
so that we may know in our lives
your saving grace and healing power
until that day when we will see you face to face,
through Jesus Christ our Lord. Amen.

or

Lord Jesus,
when you enter our lives you bring into your light
the sins we have held onto in the darkness,
and disclose the purposes of our hearts.
We confess that we have not worshipped or obeyed you as king,
nor lived as members of your kingdom.
Forgive us all our sins,
restore to us the joy of your salvation
and fill our hearts with the hope of glory
through Jesus Christ our Lord. Amen.

CHRISTMAS

Lord Jesus,
you were born in the poverty of a stable,
but we have allowed Christmas
to become an excuse for self-indulgence.
Our hearts have become dulled by materialism and selfishness
and our eyes fail to see you at work in our lives
and in our world.
**We confess that we have not responded to your love,
and have often failed to share your compassion with others.
Forgive us we pray,
and in your mercy give us a fresh vision
of that great love which longs to make us whole again,
and fresh strength to share that love with others,
for the sake of your kingdom, Amen.**

or

Lord Jesus,
Wonderful Counsellor,
you pardon us and free us from guilt.

Lord have mercy,
Lord, have mercy.

Lord Jesus,
Mighty God,
you protect us and encourage us on our way.

Christ have mercy,
Christ, have mercy.

Lord Jesus,
Prince of Peace,
you save us and heal us from all our troubles.

Lord have mercy,
Lord, have mercy.

or

Heavenly Father,
you sent your Son to this world to bring us
    into your kingdom of light,
yet we often prefer to remain in the darkness.

In your mercy,
forgive us and heal us.

Heavenly Father,
you sent your Son to this world to transform
our lives and restore us to your presence,
yet we often prefer to remain as we are.

In your mercy,
forgive us and heal us.

Heavenly Father,
you sent your Son to this world to give us the joy
    of your salvation and the hope of eternal life,
yet we often prefer to remain unaffected by them.

In your mercy,
forgive us and heal us,
so that released from the chains of sin and fear
we may rejoice with the shepherds and the angels
at the good news that our Saviour is born. Amen.

EPIPHANY

Lord Jesus,
you reveal your truth to us,
but we fail to understand
or obey your will for our lives.

Forgive our stubbornness,
and help us to see your glory.

Lord Jesus,
you reveal your compassion to us,
but we fail to demonstrate it to others.

Forgive our selfishness,
and help us to see your glory.

Lord Jesus,
you reveal your power to us,
but we prefer to trust our own strength.

Forgive our wilfulness,
and help us to see your glory.

Lord Jesus,
you reveal your heavenly Father to us,
but we remain unmoved and unchanged.

Forgive our earthbound ways,
**and help us to see your glory
more and more
until we see you face to face. Amen.**

or

Jesus, child in the manger,
you were worshipped by wise men
who travelled far to seek you
and bring costly gifts at your birth.
We too have seen your glory,
but confess that it has not moved us to worship or sacrifice.
Forgive us for selfishly holding on to what we have,
and refusing to acknowledge you as our Lord and King.
Help us to worship you in spirit and in truth
that we might reveal your glory to the world. Amen.

LENT

God our Father,
you are mighty to save but we are weak and sinful,
and have fallen away from your presence.

In your great mercy,
forgive us O Lord.

God our Father,
you are completely faithful,
but we are changeable and fickle,
and have put our trust in the things of this passing world.

In your great mercy,
forgive us, O Lord.

God our Father,
you are gracious and forgiving,
but we are critical and self-righteous,
and have not turned to you in penitence and faith.

In your great mercy,
forgive us, O Lord.

God our Father,
you are eternal and changeless,
but we are earthbound and worldly,
and have not responded to your forgiving love.
In your great mercy,
forgive us, O Lord,
take away our sin and guilt,
and give us a clearer vision
of what you would have us be,
for the glory of your Son,
our Saviour, Jesus Christ. Amen.

or

According to your unfailing love and great compassion,
blot out our transgressions, O God.

Lord, have mercy.
Lord, have mercy.

Cleanse us with hyssop, and we shall be clean;
wash us, and we shall be whiter than snow.

Christ, have mercy.
Christ, have mercy.

Restore to us the joy of your salvation
and grant us a willing spirit to sustain us.

Lord, have mercy.
Lord, have mercy.

or

Lord God,
we have done evil in your sight;
we have sinned against you alone.
We are sorry and repent.
Have mercy on us according to your love.
Wash away our wrongdoing
and cleanse us from our sin.
Renew a right spirit within us
and restore us to the joy of your salvation,
through Jesus Christ our Lord. Amen.

PASSIONTIDE

Lord Jesus,
we come to you in penitence and faith,
asking your forgiveness for our many sins and failings.

Most merciful Lord,
forgive us and heal us.

We have failed you by acting in our own strength and disobeying
    your commands,
and have not put our trust wholly in you.

Most merciful Lord,
forgive us and heal us.

We have failed you by acting out of arrogance and pride,
and have not humbled ourselves before you.

Most merciful Lord,
forgive us and heal us.

We have failed you by acting as though you had no part in
our lives,
and have not acknowledged you as Lord and King.

Most merciful Lord,
forgive us and heal us.

We have failed you by acting out of self-interest
and have not shown your compassion and love to those in need.

Most merciful Lord,
forgive us and heal us.
Turn our failings into strengths
and our weaknesses into opportunities
for the sake of your kingdom. Amen.

or

Almighty God,
your Son Jesus Christ came to be the servant of all
and to give his life as a ransom for many.
We have acted selfishly and thoughtlessly
and have not followed his way of service and sacrifice.
Cleanse us from our wrong attitudes
and heal us of narrow prejudice,
so that we may follow the example of our Saviour
and live to the glory of your name. Amen.

or

Christ died for us, leaving us an example,
that we should follow in his steps.

Lord, have mercy.
Lord, have mercy.

He bore our sins in his body on the tree,
that we might die to sin and live to righteousness.

Christ, have mercy.
Christ, have mercy.

By his wounds we have been healed.

Lord, have mercy.
Lord, have mercy.

EASTER

Living Lord,
raised from death and victorious over evil,
we come before you to confess our sins and weaknesses.

By your mighty power,
raise us to new and eternal life.

Living Lord,
by your death and resurrection
you have destroyed the power of evil,
yet we often yield to temptation.

By your mighty power deliver us from our sins,
and raise us to new and eternal life.

Living Lord,
by your resurrection you have won for us freedom and new life,
yet we often allow our lives to be dominated by guilt and fear.

By your mighty power deliver us from our sins,
and raise us to new and eternal life.

Living Lord,
by your death and resurrection you have opened up for us the
    way to eternal life,
yet we often live without thinking of our home in heaven.

By your mighty power deliver us from our sins,
and raise us to new and eternal life.
Set our minds on the things which are above,
where you reign for ever,
King of Kings and Lord of Lords. Amen.

or

Almighty God,
by whose will and power the Lord Jesus Christ was raised
    from death,
we confess that we have not always lived as those who
    believe in him.
In our rebellion we have gone our own way;
in our weakness we have stumbled and fallen;
and in our pride we have ignored your offer of forgiveness
    and restoration.
We are sorry and repent,
and ask you to pardon all our wrongdoing.
Renew our vision, we pray,
heal our wounds
and fill our hearts with the joy of Easter morning
for the sake of your Son, our risen Lord Jesus Christ. Amen.

or

Praise the Lord, O my soul, and do not forget his benefits.

Lord, have mercy.
Lord, have mercy.

He forgives all my sins and heals all my diseases.

Christ, have mercy.
Christ, have mercy.

He redeems my life from the pit,
and crowns me with love and compassion.

Lord, have mercy.
Lord, have mercy.

ASCENSIONTIDE

Lord of glory,
you left your home in heaven to share our earthly life
and die for us on Calvary.
We are sorry that we have not loved you with all our hearts.

In your mercy,
forgive us and help us.

Lord of glory,
you rose from the grave as victor over sin and death.
We are sorry that we have not lived in the light of eternal life.

In your mercy,
forgive us and help us.

Lord of glory,
you ascended into heaven where you reign for ever at the
    right hand of the Father.
We are sorry that we have not always worshipped you as
    our king.

In your mercy,
forgive us and help us.
Fill us with a new obedience to your will
and a new joy in worship,
that we may live to your praise and glory. Amen.

or

Lord Jesus Christ,
you are our great high priest who has passed into the heavens
where you now sit at the right hand of God the Father.
When we see your glory we recognise afresh our sinfulness
   and weakness,
and come to you in penitence and faith to seek your pardon.
Forgive us our sins, we pray,
and heal our waywardness.
Help us to worship you as King,
love you as Saviour
and serve you as Master
to the glory of your name. Amen.

PENTECOST

Spirit of God,
we come to you acknowledging your transforming power
and confessing our own lack of faith.

We ask you to forgive and heal us,
and fill us with your strength.

Spirit of God,
you came upon the disciples in wind and flame,
filling them with your power and authority.
We confess that our lives show little of your power within
and our witness little sign of your authority.

We ask you to forgive and heal us,
and fill us with your power.

Spirit of God,
you came upon the church to bestow gifts and blessing.
We confess that we have too often been content
with the earthbound poverty of our lives.

We ask you to forgive and heal us,
and fill us with your life.

Spirit of God,
you come upon us, your people,
to equip us for your service.
We confess that we have resisted your working within us.

We ask you to forgive and heal us,
and fill us with your love.
Renew our lives and release our tongues to declare your praise,
and reveal your glory to the world through Jesus Christ our
Lord. Amen.

or

Almighty God,
we confess that we have sinned against you
in thought, word and action.
We have grieved your Holy Spirit
and not allowed him to enter our lives
in healing and saving power.
We are sorry and repent of all that has hindered your work in
us.
Forgive us, we pray,
heal our hurts,
and fill our hearts with the fire of your love,
that we may live to your praise and glory,
for the sake of your Son,
our Saviour Jesus Christ. Amen.

FOR CHURCH UNITY

Lord of the church,
we confess to you the sins which have caused divisions among
    your people.
We have put up barriers of fear and distrust;
we have created blocks of prejudice and suspicion;
we have broken the unity Christ died to win.
We are most truly sorry and seek your forgiveness.
Replace our pride and selfishness with your peace and joy,
    we pray,
and restore us to fellowship with you and with one another;
for your holy name's sake. Amen.

GENERAL

Generous God,
we come before you recognising your loving care
    and healing power.
Forgive us, we pray,
that our own lives do not demonstrate your compassion
    or salvation.

In your mercy fill us with your love,
and make us whole.

Forgive us, we pray,
that we do not share your concern for the needy and poor.

In your mercy, fill us with your care,
and make us whole.

Forgive us, we pray,
that we are selfish with all you have given us.

In your mercy, fill us with your generosity,
and make us whole.

Forgive us, we pray,
that we are self-centred and unloving in our relationships.

In your mercy, fill us with your love,
and make us whole.
Free us from the tyranny of self
and by your Spirit help us to bring your healing love
    to all in need or distress,
for the sake of your Son Jesus Christ,
who healed all who came to him in faith. Amen.

or

Heavenly Father,
we confess that we have not loved you with all our heart,
nor our neighbours as ourselves.
We have not cared enough for you,
for your world,
or for those around us,
but have been self-satisfied and self-centred.
We are truly sorry for all our wrong attitudes and behaviour,
and ask you to forgive our sinfulness.
Help us, we pray,
to trust in your healing power,
and live as those whose lives have been transformed,
for your glory's sake. Amen.

or

Seek the Lord while he may be found.
Call upon him while he is near.

Lord, have mercy.
Lord, have mercy.

Turn to the Lord and he will have mercy,
to our God, for he will freely pardon.

Christ, have mercy.
Christ, have mercy.

You will go out with joy,
and be led forth in peace,
and the mountains and hills will burst into song before you.

Lord, have mercy.
Lord, have mercy.

or

I waited patiently for the Lord;
he turned to me and heard my cry.

Lord, have mercy.
Lord, have mercy.

He lifted me out of the slimy pit
and set my feet on a rock.

Christ, have mercy.
Christ, have mercy.

He put a new song in my mouth,
a hymn of praise to our God.

Lord, have mercy.
Lord, have mercy.

or

Lord our God,
in our sin we have avoided your call.
Our love for you is like the mist,
disappearing in the heat of the sun.
Have mercy on us.
Bind up our wounds,
and bring us back to the foot of the cross,
through Jesus Christ our Lord. Amen.

ABSOLUTIONS

ADVENT, CHRISTMAS AND EPIPHANY

May the God of all healing and forgiveness draw you to himself,
that you may behold the glory of his Son,
the Word made flesh,
and be cleansed from all your sins through Jesus Christ our
   Lord. Amen.

or

Almighty God,
who shows mercy to all who turn to him,
forgive you for all your sins and failings,
grant you his peace and joy,
and through you reveal Christ to the world to the glory of his
   name. Amen.

LENT AND HOLY WEEK

Almighty God,
whose mercy is on all who come to him in penitence and faith,
grant you pardon for all your sins,
time to repent and return to him,
and the strength to walk in his way of perfect freedom,
through Jesus Christ our Lord. Amen.

or

May the God of forgiveness show you his mercy,
forgive you your sins,
and bring you to everlasting life,
through Jesus Christ our Lord. Amen.

Easter, Ascension and Pentecost

Almighty God,
who raised from the dead our Lord Jesus,
forgive you all your sins,
raise you from the death of sin to the life of righteousness,
and strengthen you to walk with him in joy and confidence,
through Jesus Christ our Lord. Amen.

or

Almighty God,
the Father of our Lord Jesus Christ,
pardon and deliver you from all your sin,
that you may live in accordance with his will
and reign with him in heaven,
to his praise and glory. Amen.

or

Almighty God,
whose Spirit comes upon all who will receive him,
grant unto you forgiveness for your sins,
peace in your hearts,
and power to live for him day by day,
through Jesus Christ our Lord. Amen.

For Church Unity

Almighty God,
who forgives all who truly repent,
have mercy upon you,
pardon and deliver you from all your sins,
and by his Spirit make you one with each other and with him;
through Jesus Christ our Lord. Amen.

General

May the God of love bring you back to himself,
forgive you your sins,
and assure you of his eternal love in Jesus Christ our Lord.
Amen.

or

Almighty God,
whose arms of mercy are always open to those
    who confess their sins,
have mercy upon you,
cleanse you from all that is wrong,
and restore you to himself for the sake of his Son,
our Saviour Jesus Christ. Amen.

or

God, the Father of all mercies,
forgive you all that makes you unworthy of him,
grant you on this earth peace and freedom from guilt,
and in the life to come eternal joy,
through Jesus Christ our Lord. Amen.

or

Almighty God have mercy upon you,
and by his great power deliver you from the forces of darkness
    into his kingdom of light, for his name's sake. Amen.

RESPONSORIAL WORDS OF PRAISE

RESPONSIVE WORDS of praise have been around for as long as people have been praising God. Many of the Psalms were written so that the congregation of God's people could corporately give him praise. Many of the following selection are based on words from the Psalter, though other parts of the Bible are included too. These can be particularly valuable as an act of praise where the worship is to contain no singing (possibly because of small numbers or lack of musicians). However, they can equally be used in larger services in which congregational participation could potentially become stifled. They could be inserted at various points during the liturgy; for example, after the Confession and Absolution in a non-Eucharistic service, or after Communion has been received in a eucharistic service.

I will praise you, O Lord, with all my heart,
I will tell of all your wonders.
You have upheld my right and my cause;
you have sat on your throne,
judging righteously.
I will praise you, O Lord, with all my heart,
I will tell of all your wonders.

You have rebuked the nations
and destroyed the wicked;
you have blotted out their name for ever.
I will praise you, O Lord, with all my heart,
I will tell of all your wonders.

You reign for ever;
you have established your throne for judgment.
I will praise you, O Lord, with all my heart,
I will tell of all your wonders.

You will judge the world in righteousness;
you will govern the peoples with justice.
I will praise you, O Lord, with all my heart,
I will tell of all your wonders.
I trust in your unfailing love;
my heart rejoices in your salvation.

Based on Psalm 9

O Lord my God, I called to you for help
    and you healed me.
You brought me up from the grave;
you spared me from going down to the pit.
O Lord my God, I called to you for help
and you healed me.

Your anger lasts only for a moment;
but your favour for a lifetime.
**O Lord my God, I called to you for help
and you healed me.**

You turned my mourning into dancing;
you removed my sackcloth and clothed me with joy.
**O Lord my God, I called to you for help
    and you healed me.
Let my heart sing to you and not be silent,
for I will give you thanks for ever.**

Based on Psalm 30

The word of the Lord is right and true;
he is faithful in all he does.
**Sing joyfully to the Lord, you righteous.
Sing to him a new song.**

The Lord loves righteousness and justice;
the earth is full of his unfailing love.
**Sing joyfully to the Lord, you righteous.
Sing to him a new song.**

The plans of the Lord stand firm for ever;
the purposes of his heart are through all generations.
**Sing joyfully to the Lord, you righteous.
Sing to him a new song.**

Based on Psalm 33

The eyes of the Lord are on the righteous;
His ears are attentive to their cry.

The righteous cry out and the Lord hears them;
He delivers them from all their troubles.

The Lord is close to the broken-hearted;
He saves those who are crushed in spirit.

Based on Psalm 34

Your love, O Lord, reaches to the heavens,
your faithfulness to the skies.
Continue your love to those who know you.

Your righteousness is like the mighty mountains,
your justice like the great deep.
Continue your love to those who know you.

We feast in the abundance of your house,
and drink from your river of delights.
Continue your love to those who know you.

With you is the fountain of life,
and in your light we see light.
Continue your love to those who know you,
and your righteousness to the upright in heart.

Based on Psalm 36

I cry out to God who fulfils his purpose for me;
he sends his love and his faithfulness.
Be exalted, O God, above the heavens;
let your glory be over all the earth.

My heart is steadfast, O my God;
I will sing and make music.
Be exalted, O God, above the heavens;
let your glory be over all the earth.

Great is your love, reaching to the heavens;
your faithfulness reaches to the skies.
Be exalted, O God, above the heavens;
let your glory be over all the earth.

Based on Psalm 57

My mouth will tell of your righteousness;
of your salvation all day long.

I will come and proclaim your mighty acts;
I will proclaim your righteousness alone.

To this day I declare your marvellous deeds;
I declare your power to the next generation.

Based on Psalm 71

I will remember the deeds of the Lord;
I will remember your miracles of long ago.

I will meditate on all your works;
I will consider all your mighty acts.

You are the God who performs miracles;
You display your power among the peoples.

Based on Psalm 77

Sing to the Lord, and praise his name;
proclaim his salvation day after day.
Sing to the Lord a new song.

Declare his glory among the nations;
his marvellous deeds among all peoples.
Sing to the Lord all the earth.

Great is the Lord and most worthy of praise;
he is to be feared more than all gods.
Sing to the Lord a new song.

Splendour and majesty are before him;
strength and glory are in his sanctuary.
Sing to the Lord all the earth.

Ascribe to the Lord the glory due to his name;
worship him in the splendour of his holiness.
Sing to the Lord a new song;
sing to the Lord all the earth.

Based on Psalm 96

The Lord works righteousness and justice
   for all who are oppressed;
Praise the Lord, O my soul.

The Lord is compassionate and gracious,
slow to anger and abounding in love;
Praise the Lord, O my soul.

The Lord does not treat us as our sins deserve,
or repay us according to our iniquities.
Praise the Lord, O my soul.

Based on Psalm 103

The Lord is gracious and righteous,
full of compassion.
I love the Lord for he heard my voice;
he heard my cry for mercy.

The Lord protects the simple-hearted;
when I was in great need he saved me.
I love the Lord for he heard my voice;
he heard my cry for mercy.

The Lord has been good to you,
O my soul; be at rest once more.
I love the Lord for he heard my voice;
he heard my cry for mercy.

Based on Psalm 116

I will bow down towards your holy temple
and praise your name for your love and faithfulness.
I will praise you, O Lord, with all my heart.

When I called, you answered me;
you made me bold and strong in heart.
I will praise you, O Lord, with all my heart.

Though I walk in the midst of trouble you preserve my life;
with your right hand you save me.
I will praise you, O Lord, with all my heart.

Based on Psalm 138

How good it is to sing praises to our God;
**For he heals the broken-hearted
and binds up their wounds.**

How good it is to sing praises to our God;
**For he is mighty in power,
and his understanding has no limit.**

How good it is to sing praises to our God;
For he delights in those who put their hope in his unfailing love.
Based on Psalm 147

To us a child is born, to us a son is given;
the government will be upon his shoulders.
**The people walking in darkness
have seen a great light.**

He will be called Wonderful Counsellor, Mighty God,
Everlasting Father, the Prince of Peace.
**The people walking in darkness
have seen a great light.**

Of the increase of his government and peace
there will be no end.
**The people walking in darkness
have seen a great light.**
Based on Isaiah 9

Every valley shall be raised up,
every mountain and hill made low.
'Comfort, comfort my people,' says the Lord.

The rough ground shall become level,
the rugged places a plain.
'Comfort, comfort my people,' says the Lord.

The glory of the Lord shall be revealed;
all mankind together will see it.
'Comfort, comfort my people,' says the Lord.

Based on Isaiah 40

How beautiful on the mountains are the feet
  of those who bring good news,
who proclaim peace and salvation;
Say to his people, 'Your God reigns.'

Burst into songs of joy together,
for the Lord has comforted his people;
Say to his people, 'Your God reigns.'

All the ends of the earth
  will see the salvation of our God;
Say to his people, 'Your God reigns.'

Based on Isaiah 52

Praise the Lord, the God of Israel,
for he has come and redeemed his people.

He has given us salvation from our enemies,
from the hand of those who hate us;
Praise the Lord, the God of Israel,
for he has come and redeemed his people.

He has shown mercy to our ancestors,
and remembered his holy covenant.
Praise the Lord, the God of Israel,
for he has come and redeemed his people.

He has rescued us from our enemies,
and enabled us to serve him without fear
in holiness and righteousness all our days.
Praise the Lord, the God of Israel,
for he has come and redeemed his people.

Based on Luke 1

Alleluia! Salvation and glory
   and power belong to our God;
True and just are his judgments.

Alleluia! Praise our God,
   all you his servants;
You who fear him, both small and great.

Alleluia! Our Lord God almighty reigns;
Let us rejoice and be glad and give him glory.

Based on Revelation 19

Christ Jesus, being in very nature God,
did not consider equality with God something to be grasped;
He made himself nothing,
taking the very nature of a servant.

He humbled himself and became
obedient to death on a cross;
Therefore God has exalted him
to the highest place.

At the name of Jesus every knee shall bow,
in heaven and on earth and under the earth.
And every tongue confess
that Jesus Christ is Lord,
to the glory of God the Father.

Based on Philippians 2

INTERCESSIONS

IN A healing service of any kind, the main focus will be on the prayer for individuals which is accompanied by the laying on of hands. However, that should not mean that the intercessions are reduced in significance. It is in the nature of a healing service that a fair amount of attention will be given to the personal needs and concerns of the worshippers, so the corporate prayer expressed in the intercessions is an opportunity to prevent them from becoming too self-absorbed and inward-looking. However they are structured, intercessions should cover the needs of the wider church and the world around, as well as mentioning particular individuals. Recognising the greater needs of others often contributes to the healing process and in any event engenders a sense of gratitude to God. We are not presenting God with a 'shopping-list' of things we want him to do for us. Rather, we are bringing to him situations beyond our control or understanding and opening them up to the work of his Holy Spirit, not demanding a set answer, but leaving the concern in his loving hands.

The following intercessions are responsive, and give opportunity for local concerns and needs to be articulated, as well as any national or international situations which may be on people's minds at the time of the service.

ADVENT

Creator God,
you formed the world from chaos and darkness,
and brought into being its beauty and grandeur.
Help us to be good stewards
   of what you have entrusted to us,
and to show your hope in places
   where there is hurt and despair.

God of all hope,
hear your people's prayer.

Provider God,
you sustain us day by day;
all that we have comes from your good hand.
Help us to show our gratitude to you
   both in word and action,
and to work so that everyone
   may receive your gracious provision.

God of all goodness,
hear your people's prayer.

Redeemer God,
you come to us in your Son Jesus Christ,
the Light of the world,
bringing joy and peace to those
   whose lives are filled with sadness or conflict.
Help us to share the good news of your saving love
   with the fearful, the lonely and the rejected,
so that they may find in you strength and security.

God of all grace,
hear your people's prayer.

Sovereign God,
you will come again in glory to judge the world
    and take your people to yourself.
Help us so to live that we will
    at all times be ready to meet you,
and keep our eyes fixed on things eternal
until that day when we see you face to face.

God of all glory,
hear your people's prayer
and grant them in this life peace,
and in the life to come eternal joy
for the sake of your Kingdom. Amen.

CHRISTMAS

As we kneel with the shepherds before the Christ child
we bring him our prayers and requests saying,

Jesus, eternal Word,
be born in us today.

Lord Jesus,
you are the Wonderful Counsellor who calls us
into fellowship with our heavenly Father and one another.
May we, your people, be one with you
    and with each other,
as we seek to bring your healing and peace
    to a broken and needy world.
We pray for the church in . . .

Jesus, eternal Word,
be born in us today.

Lord Jesus,
you are the Mighty God who came from your home
    in glory to share our sorrows and joys.
May we, your people, worship you as king
and serve you as Lord,
so that the world may come to acknowledge
    the healing power of your just and gentle rule.
We pray for the leaders of the nations . . .

Jesus, Eternal Word,
be born in us today.

Lord Jesus,
you are the everlasting Father
and welcome your children with open arms
when they return to you and seek your face.
May we, your people, turn again to you
    in penitence and faith,
and in our words and deeds lift you up,
so that all people might be drawn into your healing presence.
We pray for those who do not recognise you as Lord . . .

Jesus, eternal Word,
be born in us today.

Lord Jesus,
you are the Prince of Peace who brings comfort
    and security to those who are anxious and sorrowful.
May we, your people, experience the healing
    and peace you alone can give,
and reflect this in the way we live day by day.
We pray for those who particularly need your healing touch
    on their lives in body, mind or spirit . . .

Jesus, eternal Word,
be born in us today,
and help us to share in your unending life,
because we ask it in your name. Amen.

EPIPHANY

As we see the radiance of Christ our Saviour, we pray,

Lord Jesus, Light of the world,
shine in the darkness, we pray.

You are the Light of lights
and in you there is no darkness at all.
Help us to live in the light of your holiness
so that others may be drawn into your glorious presence.
We pray for the church,
that it may reveal to the world
   the light of your love . . .

Lord Jesus, Light of the world,
shine in the darkness, we pray.

You are a light to the nations,
and the glory of your people.
Help us to live in the light of your example,
and uphold your justice and peace.
We pray for you to heal the world,
and guide those who influence the course of events . . .

Lord Jesus, Light of the world,
Shine in the darkness, we pray.

You are the light which has not been overcome
    by the world and surrounding darkness.
Help us to reflect your light in the dark areas of life
and banish the shadows of sin, death and disease.
We pray for those we know whose lives are made gloomy
    through illness, disease or injury . . .

Lord Jesus, Light of the world,
Shine in the darkness, we pray,
and reveal your glory to all mankind. Amen.

LENT

We come before Christ our Saviour
trusting in his mercy and saying,

Lord, in your mercy,
hear our prayer.

We bring to the mercy of Christ
    the church and God's people throughout the world.
Especially we pray . . .
May we with them bear witness to your saving love.

Lord in your mercy,
hear our prayer.

We bring to the mercy of Christ
    our world, those who govern it,
    and those who suffer in it.
Especially we pray . . .
May we bear witness to your compassion and healing.

Lord in your mercy,
hear our prayer.

We bring to the mercy of Christ
    our families and friends,
    and those whose lives touch ours,
    at work or at home.
Especially we pray . . .
May we bear witness to your forgiving grace.

Lord in your mercy,
hear our prayer.

We bring to the mercy of Christ
    anyone known to us who is suffering through illness,
    sadness or loneliness.
Especially we pray . . .
May we bear witness to your healing power.

Lord in your mercy,
hear our prayer.

We bring to the mercy of Christ our own lives.
May we bear witness to your coming kingdom.

Lord in your mercy,
hear our prayer,
and graciously answer us when we call upon you,
for the sake of your holy name. Amen.

HOLY WEEK

We bring our prayers to Jesus,
who was despised and rejected,
saying,

Lord of love,
hear our cry.

Lord Jesus,
you were criticised and condemned by those
    who could not stand in the light of your presence.
We pray for all your people who suffer ridicule
    or ill-treatment for their faith,
especially . . .
May they stand firm in their faith
and remain joyful in their hope.

Lord of love,
hear our cry.

Lord Jesus,
you were arrested wrongly and tried unfairly.
We pray for all who suffer as a result
    of injustice and oppression,
especially . . .
May they be given courage and patience
    to be true to themselves and true to you.

Lord of love,
hear our cry.

Lord Jesus,
you were mocked and jeered by the crowds
and flogged by the authorities.
We pray for all who suffer physical or mental abuse,
especially . . .
May they receive comfort and assurance
    in their troubles and healing for their pain.

Lord of love,
hear our cry.

Lord Jesus,
you were hung on the cross as a criminal,
and bore the agony of death in your own body.
We pray for all who suffer pain in their bodies or minds,
especially . . .
May they receive the healing which comes
    only from the wounds inflicted on you.

Lord of love,
hear our cry.

Lord Jesus,
you were utterly alone as you died,
taking on yourself the sins or the whole world.
We pray for all who suffer through loneliness and isolation . . .
May they find in you the faithful friend
    who will never leave them or let them down.

Lord of love,
hear our cry,
and help us all to experience
the wonder of your healing
and the joy of your salvation,
to the glory of your holy name. Amen.

EASTER

In confidence we bring our prayers and requests
    to our living Lord, saying,

Risen Master,
in your mercy, hear us.

We ask you to fill us and your whole church
    with the power of your resurrection life.
May we all fulfil together your great commission
    to preach the gospel and make disciples of all nations.
We pray for the church in . . .

Risen Master
in your mercy, hear us.

We ask you to fill us
    with the truth of your resurrection life.
May we be given boldness to declare
    the good news of eternal life
    to those who have not heard it.
We pray for all who bear witness to you . . .

Risen Master,
in your mercy, hear us.

We ask you to fill us
    with the peace of your resurrection life.
May we bring that peace to a world
    full of violence and conflict.
We pray for all who suffer as a result of warfare,
    exploitation or injustice . . .

Risen Master,
in your mercy, hear us.

We ask you to fill us
   with the healing of your resurrection life.
May we share your healing grace
   with those around who endure pain
   and ill-health in body or mind.
We pray for those known to us
   who are suffering as a result of
   disease or injury,
   anxiety or grief,
   sadness or distress . . .

Risen Master,
in your mercy, hear us.

We ask you to fill us
   with the joy of your resurrection life.
May we proclaim your praise
   with our lips and in our lives.

Risen Master,
in your mercy,
hear us and receive our prayers
which we offer to the living God,
and ask in the name of his risen Son. Amen.

ASCENSIONTIDE

Let us pray to the King of Kings
   enthroned on high, saying,

Lord of glory,
hear your people's prayer.

Jesus, Lord of all,
you are worthy to receive glory and honour and power,
for you created all things.
We ask you to restore and heal your creation,
ravaged and spoiled by human selfishness and greed.
In the way we treat our environment and other people
may we show your care and provision in all our relationships . . .

Lord of glory,
hear your people's prayer.

Jesus, Lord of all,
you are worthy to receive wisdom and strength
for by your blood you have purchased people for God
   from every nation and race.
We ask you to restore and heal the nations of the world,
torn apart by hatred and fear and violence.
May we show your justice and righteousness in the world . . .

Lord of glory,
hear your people's prayer.

Jesus, Lord of all,
you are worthy to receive praise for ever and ever
for you have made us a kingdom
   of priests to serve our God.
We ask you to restore and heal your Church,
troubled by division and disunity.
May we put aside our differences,
recognising that we are one in you,
and reveal your glory to the world . . .

Lord of glory,
Hear your people's prayer.
May we fall down before your throne
   and worship you,
the Lamb who was slain,
for ever and ever. Amen.

PENTECOST

We wait for the power from on high
   to come upon us as we pray,

Lord, bless us and heal us,
and fill us with your Spirit.

Holy Spirit,
we ask you to fill us with your power,
that we may be strengthened to serve you better.
May we be bold to proclaim your salvation and healing,
and to minister in your name . . .

Lord, bless us and heal us,
and fill us with your power.

Holy Spirit,
we ask you to fill us with your wisdom,
that we may understand better your purposes in our lives.
May we see more clearly
   how you call us to live in this world . . .

Lord, bless us and heal us,
and fill us with your wisdom.

Holy Spirit, we ask you to fill us with your gifts
that we may be equipped to work better for you.
May we discern the ministries
   we have been called to in your name . . .

Lord, bless us and heal us,
and fill us with your gifts.

Holy Spirit,
we ask you to fill us with your peace,
that we may be confident of your love in every situation.
May we be able to share that peace
   with all in particular need . . .

Lord, bless us and heal us,
and fill us with your peace.

Holy Spirit,
fill us with your love,
that we may bring your care and compassion
   to all in need or distress.
May our words and our lives demonstrate your love
   whatever you call us to be . . .

Lord, bless us and heal us,
and fill us with your love.
Make us one in heart and mind
to serve you for the glory of Christ our Lord. Amen.

GENERAL

Lord Jesus,
you healed the lame and enabled them to walk again.
May we also rejoice at your power to heal and restore,
and run to serve you with willing feet.
We pray for your people, the church . . .

Lord of all healing,
grant us your wholeness.

Lord Jesus,
you healed the blind and restored their vision.
May we also rejoice to know that now we can see,
and look for every opportunity to serve you
    and bear witness to your healing power.
We pray for your world, which we are called to serve . . .

Lord of all healing,
grant us your vision.

Lord Jesus,
you healed the lepers
and brought them back into their community.
May we also rejoice in your care for the outcast
and seek to bring them within your arms of love.
We pray for the rejected and lonely,
and all who feel unloved or unwanted . . .

Lord of all healing,
grant us your compassion.

Lord Jesus,
you healed the sorrowful and sad,
and gave them hope and joy.

May we also rejoice in the new life you offer
    and share your love with all whose lives are
    scarred by unhappiness or anxiety.
We pray for any known to us . . .

Lord of all healing,
grant us your love,
that we may fulfil your commission to heal the sick
for the glory of your kingdom. Amen.

or

Lord Jesus,
you showed compassion to all who came
    to you in illness or distress.
Hear our prayers
    for those who need your healing touch in any way.

Loving Lord Jesus,
heal us we pray.

We bring to you the needs of the world.
Heal all who suffer through hunger, poverty,
    fear or oppression, especially . . .

Loving Lord Jesus,
heal your world we pray.

We bring to you our divided church.
Heal our conflicts and divisions,
and help us to live in the unity you died to bring.
Especially . . .

Loving Lord Jesus,
heal your church we pray.

(continued overleaf)

We bring to you our families and friends.
Heal damaged relationships
   and breathe your peace into our lives.
Especially . . .

Loving Lord Jesus,
heal our homes we pray.

We bring to you those known to us
   who are ill or suffering in any way.
Heal them in body, mind and spirit
and meet their deepest needs . . .

Loving Lord Jesus,
heal our friends we pray.

We bring to you ourselves.
Heal our fear and sadness
and fill our hearts with your eternal love and joy.

Loving Lord Jesus,
Heal us all we pray,
and help us live in your strength alone,
to your praise and glory. Amen.

WORDS OF BLESSING

THE FOLLOWING short group of blessings are intended to be used at the laying on of hands and for anointing with oil. They can be varied to suit particular circumstances and occasions, but do not constitute an alternative 'soft option' to specific prayer – if this does not form part of the service it should certainly be available afterwards for any who want it. All of the following can be used by those ministering healing, ordained or lay, and are based firmly on Trinitarian theology. It is vital for those receiving this ministry to understand that whoever is exercising it does so only under the authority of the church and in the name of Christ.

May you be filled in body, mind and spirit
with the healing power of the Holy Spirit of Jesus.

May Christ, the Son of God, by the power of his Holy Spirit,
heal you of all your infirmities and anxieties.

May you know the healing love of Christ in every part of your life
through the power of his Holy Spirit.

May you know the blessing of God, Father, Son and Holy Spirit,
as you kneel before him in faith and expectancy.

May the love of the Father, the grace of the Lord Jesus,
and the joy of the Holy Spirit
fill your heart and mind now and for ever.

May you know the joy of sins forgiven,
the peace which passes all understanding
and the hope of eternal life
as you are filled with the healing power of the Holy Spirit
of Jesus.

May God's healing power fill your life and make you whole
    as you respond to the love of Christ
      through his Holy Spirit at work within you.

May your mind be open, your heart warmed
    and your hands outstretched
    to receive the healing power
    of the Holy Spirit of Jesus into your life.

May the grace of our Lord Jesus Christ draw you to the Father;
may the love of the Father open your heart to the work of the
    Holy Spirit;
and may the peace of the Holy Spirit heal you of all anxieties
    and diseases as you come before him.

May you be healed and made whole by God,
the Father, the Son and the Holy Spirit,
and leave this place in newness of life to the honour of his name.

May the love of God be poured out upon you
as you receive his healing touch.

May God, who through the resurrection of his Son Jesus Christ
gives us the victory,
give you joy, peace and healing grace
as you walk with him day by day.

FURTHER PRAYERS

THE GREAT advantage of responsorial prayers is that they enable the congregational to participate actively in the intercessions. Their disadvantage is that it is not always possible to direct them to specific concerns. Bidding prayers can be said either by the minister or by the whole congregation, and have the benefit of being easily focussed on a particular area of need. Equally they can be more general in tone. They can be included at many different points in the service apart from the intercessions, for example at the beginning of a service, or after Communion.

The following selection of prayers covers a variety of seasons and circumstances. Some are clearly intercessory, others could be used in a number of ways. They are also easy to adapt to particular local needs.

ADVENT

Lord Jesus Christ,
we look forward expectantly to your coming again in glory
    and rejoice in the hope you have set before us.
You will come as saviour,
    to bring all those who love and serve you
    into your glorious kingdom;
as king, to bring all nations and their rulers under your authority;
as judge, to bring justice to our world.
May we worship and love you as our saviour;
serve you gladly as our king;
and so live for others on this earth,
that in the world to come you will receive us
    as those who have ministered your healing and compassion.
We ask this for the sake of your kingdom. Amen.

CHRISTMAS

Lord Jesus, King of Glory,
you were born in a stable as one of us;
grew up in an ordinary family like us;
and shared all our sorrows and joys.
You had no home of your own
    and knew what it means to be poor.
We bring before you all who today live in poverty or misery:
    the homeless, who have nowhere to eat or sleep;
    the unemployed, who have no way of earning their living;
    the exploited, whose lives are made unbearable
    through squalid housing, lack of opportunities,
    and the selfishness of others.
We pray that you will give us grateful hearts
    for your goodness to us,
and fill those same hearts with your compassion,
that we may be willing to live simply
so that others may simply live.
We ask this for your glory. Amen.

EPIPHANY

Lord Jesus, Light of the world,
    shine in the darkness that surrounds us, we pray.
Many are suffering through illness, loneliness or bereavement,
    while others endure the pain of hardship and exploitation.
May your glorious light dawn on those whose hearts are
    full of anxiety, sorrow, grief or distress
    and bring healing to them in body, mind or spirit.
May our lives so demonstrate the power of your kingdom,
    that others will come to experience your transforming love
    for themselves,
for your glory's sake. Amen.

LENT

Lord Jesus Christ,
    you are the great healer who gave sight to the blind,
    hearing to the deaf,
    and peace to the fearful.
We ask you to open our eyes to the level of need around;
    our ears to hear what you say;
    and our hearts to the peace and joy which you alone can give.
May we be able to discern problems as they are presented
    and deal with them sensitively.
May we learn to act only in accordance with your will;
    and may our hearts be filled with your love and care
    as we seek to bring others into your kingdom.
We pray that our lives may be so touched by your healing power
    that others who do not know you may come to rejoice
    in your saving grace for your glory's sake. Amen.

HOLY WEEK

Lord God,
    you sent your Son Jesus Christ to dwell among us,
    living as one of us and sharing our sorrows and joys.
He was tempted in every way as we are yet without sin,
    and will save completely all those who come to him in faith.
We pray for your healing touch on those who are anxious,
    sorrowful or bowed down with the burdens of life.
May they experience your power afresh,
    recognising that your strength is made perfect in weakness.
Heal their hurts, we ask you,
    make them whole again
    and restore them to full health
    in body, mind and spirit,
to live and work to your praise and glory. Amen.

EASTER

Almighty God,
    by your great power you brought your Son Jesus Christ
    back from death to new and unending life.
By his obedience to you he has conquered the grave,
    broken the chains of sin for ever,
    and given us a hope for the future which cannot
    be taken away.
We ask you to bless and heal all who need your
    comforting and sustaining presence,
    whether they are lonely, anxious or oppressed.
May they be released from fear of death,
    from slavery to guilt,
    and grant them the assurance of sins forgiven
    and life for evermore,
for the sake of Jesus Christ our Lord. Amen.

ASCENSIONTIDE

Lord Jesus Christ,
risen and reigning King,
you have overcome all the forces of evil
    by your death and resurrection,
and sit at the right hand of God the Father interceding for us.
We pray for all who are in despair,
who have no hope for the future,
and who feel helpless in the face of the pressures
    they have to endure day by day.
May they find in you the great high priest
    who has experienced every kind of human sorrow,
and receive from you the healing which flows
    to them from your wounds.
May they too, with us, acknowledge you as Saviour and Lord
and gladly bow the knee before your throne for the sake of
your glory. Amen.

PENTECOST

Holy Spirit of Jesus,
you visited the disciples in the upper room
in the form of wind and fire,
filling them with power and boldness
    to proclaim the good news and heal the sick.
We ask you to come into our lives
and fill us with that same divine energy
    to bring the joy of your salvation to all people,
and especially to those whose need is more acute at the moment.
Make us channels of your love and grace,
and as we bear witness to the truth of the gospel,
may those who come to us receive your blessing and healing.
We ask this that your name may be glorified
and your kingdom extended. Amen.

FOR DOCTORS AND NURSES

Heavenly Father,
you have created us
and our health and strength are gifts from you.
You sustain us and provide for us day by day,
but equip and enable us to be stewards of this earth for you.
We thank you for your provision of medicine to make us well,
and for those who have the gift of bringing bodily healing
    through medication and surgery.
Bless doctors and nurses,
and all others whose work contributes to the care of the sick
    or injured,
and to restoring their health.
In their decisions may they act responsibly,
recognising that you alone have power over life and death;
in their tasks may they work willingly,
despite the pressures which bear upon them;
and in their care may they demonstrate the love
    and compassion of Jesus,
who healed all who came to him in faith.
This we ask in his name and for his sake. Amen.

FOR RELATIONSHIPS

Lord Jesus,
you lived in a family at Nazareth and know well
    the pressures and tensions which arise from time to time in
    the home.
We ask you to heal all whose lives are suffering
    as a result of poor or fractured relationships,
and to bring them harmony and peace
instead of anger and bitterness.
May they trust you even when they have little faith in anyone else
and allow you to overcome their resentment by the power of
    your love,
for the sake of your kingdom. Amen.

For Carers and Helpers

Lord Jesus,
there is no end to your compassion,
and no-one who came to you for healing was ever turned away.
We bring before you all who care for loved ones
   on a long-term basis,
and ask you to give them strength and courage
   to continue their work of helping those whose weakness of
   body or mind prevents them from taking a full part in life.
In the everyday routines of their homes
   may they display your joy, and in the frustrating times
   may they show forth your patience,
   affirming the value before you of every human being,
   whatever their background, status or state of health.
Above all fill their hearts with the love of our Saviour
Jesus Christ,
in whose name we pray this. Amen.

For Counsellors

Lord Jesus,
you listened with care to all who came to you
   with their problems and difficulties
and never turned them away.
We remember before you all who are engaged in the work of
   counselling,
meeting people with health problems or family difficulties
and seeking to help them come to terms with a particular
   situation.
Grant them insight and sensitivity in their tasks we pray,
and the gift of discernment to see what the real needs and
   issues are,
so that those who come to them may be given help and comfort,
and above all be drawn into your loving presence,
there to find healing and freedom, for your name's sake.
Amen.

FOR THOSE SUFFERING FROM
DEPRESSION OR ANXIETY

Lord Jesus,
alone in Gethsemane and forsaken by your friends,
you faced the agony of crucifixion and death,
obeying the Father's will and enduring pain and suffering
    so that we might be made whole.
We ask you to bless all whose inner lives are in turmoil and crisis,
or who feel they just cannot cope with the surrounding
    pressures and difficulties.
May they find you to be the Light of the world,
who shines in the darkness of their depression and fear,
and rest in your unchanging love.
Help them to recognise their need of your healing touch,
and to open their lives to receive your blessing,
that they may be restored to full health again
in body, mind and spirit. Amen.

FOR HEALING COMMUNITIES AND CENTRES

We thank you, heavenly Father
    for the work of Christian healing centres.
Inspired and strengthened by your Spirit,
    and under your guidance,
        may they be havens of your peace and tranquillity
        in all the pressure and busy-ness of the world around.
Bless those who work in them,
ministering healing in your name and providing environments
    for healing,
and enable them to bring your kingdom
    to the suffering and needy,
for your glory's sake. Amen.

For the Terminally Ill
and Those Near Death

Father God,
you are the first and the last,
and you alone know the beginning from the end.
We pray for all whose lives are approaching their close
    or whose condition has no known cure (especially . . .).
May they know the peace of your Holy Spirit
    which overcomes human despair,
and your perfect love which casts out all fear,
putting their trust in Christ,
who by his death has conquered death
    and opened the gate to everlasting life.
In his name we pray this. Amen.

For Hospices and Those Who Work in Them

Lord God,
we thank you for the work of hospices
    and for the care and commitment of those who work there.
We ask you to bless them as they seek to make the last days
    of their patients more comfortable and pleasant.
Grant them fulfilment and contentment in the tasks
    they undertake,
and may those in their care enjoy the final period of their lives
    in an atmosphere of happiness and peace.
Above all may they be places where your love is evident
    and your Spirit in control,
so that death may not be the end
    but the start of eternal life,
which is ours through the resurrection of your Son,
Jesus Christ our Lord. Amen.

FOR THE MENTALLY ILL

Loving Father,
you know us right through and understand our deepest feelings.
We pray for all who suffer
    as a result of mental illness or handicap,
that they may know the light of your presence
and the peace which passes all understanding.
Meet them in their need
and speak to them in the depths of their being,
that they may know you love and accept them as they are.
Help us to recognise their needs
and to give them a sense of their worth,
so that they may reach their full potential,
for your name's sake. Amen.

FOR ACCIDENT VICTIMS

Heavenly Father,
we pray for all whose lives have been scarred through being
    involved in an accident;
for those whose injuries are so severe that they may never live
    normally again;
for those whose actions caused the accident and are troubled
    in conscience;
for those suffering from the psychological effects and trauma;
and for those who have been shattered by the loss of a loved one.
Heal them, we ask you, from the physical and mental effects
    of what has happened to them,
enable them to come to terms with it
and bring them out from their present distress
    into the joy of your salvation through Christ our Lord. Amen.

For Aids and HIV Sufferers

Father in heaven,
we bring before you those suffering from AIDS
and those who know they are HIV positive.
Speak to them in their fear,
and bring them hope and joy by your presence
so that they may know they are not alone.
Take away any attitudes of criticism or condemnation,
whether in us or in others,
and help them to know they are accepted as they are,
both by you and by us.
Bless them and draw them close to yourself, we pray,
in the name of Jesus, who healed those whom others feared
    and rejected. Amen.

For Children at Risk

Lord Jesus Christ,
you rebuked the disciples when they turned little children
    away from you,
and instead you called them to your side.
We pray for all children,
and especially the most vulnerable and easily exploited,
the victims of physical or mental abuse,
and those left to fend for themselves.
At this impressionable age we ask you to heal them from the
    after-effects of such treatment and circumstances
    and to provide for them an environment of love and security
    in which they can grow up unhindered by the sadness of what
    has happened to them.
May we be committed to their physical welfare
    and spiritual nurture,
and enable them to deepen their faith in you,
their Saviour and friend. Amen.

For Those Engaged in Medical Research

Almighty God,
we thank you for giving us the means and resources
   to bring healing to the sick;
for those who minister in your name,
and for those whose work in hospital or surgery,
pharmacy or nursing home,
contributes to your work of making people whole.
May those who are in any way agents of your healing power
   see that their authority comes only from you,
     and that their contribution to the healing process can never
     go against your will.
We ask for your blessing to rest on all who are involved in
   medical research to discover new drugs, treatments and
   techniques.
Guide them by your wise Spirit in the ethical aspects of their
   work, as well as the practical,
so that all who are unwell or injured may benefit from it.
Remove from them the temptation to put profit
   or success above human considerations.
May this be done in the name of the Lord Jesus,
who healed every kind of disease and infirmity,
and in the power of your Spirit. Amen.

For the Elderly

Father in heaven,
no-one is beyond the scope of your care and compassion,
and there is a special place in your heart
    for the poor and vulnerable,
for those less able to look after themselves.
We pray for the elderly who are shut in,
sometimes for days at a time,
sometimes weak and open to exploitation,
afraid of the pain and immobility of old age
and worried about the loss of their independence.
You care about them
    as much as about any other age-group,
because your love transcends age differences,
and brings together young and old.
Help us to respect the older members of our community,
recognising the wisdom of their years
and enabling them to contribute to its life.
May we take your care to those who are housebound
    or in need of help,
and give them the opportunity of responding to your love,
 seen in the person and work of your Son,
our Saviour and healer, Jesus Christ. Amen.

General

Almighty and eternal God,
there is no disease of body and soul beyond the scope of your
    healing love.
May those who are sick know the power of your love
and by your mercy be restored
    to serve you afresh in holiness of living.
This we ask for the sake of your glory. Amen.

FOR CHURCH UNITY

Heavenly Father,
you gave us your Son Jesus Christ
that through his death and resurrection
we might live in harmony
   with you and with one another.
We ask for your strength, to break down the barriers of fear
   and prejudice which have divided your church;
for your love,
that we may count the well-being of others above our own;
for your peace,
to be the controlling factor in everything we do;
and for your joy
to fill our hearts as we seek to serve you together;
for the sake of your kingdom. Amen.

or

Lord Jesus,
on the night before you died
you prayed for your disciples and all who follow you,
that they might be one as you and your Father are one.
May we demonstrate that unity in all we do,
that the scars of past divisions may be healed;
that together with all Christians
   we may willingly serve your kingdom;
and that the world around might be drawn more deeply
   into your eternal love as it is seen in our lives,
for your glory's sake. Amen.

READINGS AND HYMNS

Suggested Bible Readings
and Hymns

THE CHOICE of readings and hymns is probably going to depend on what a particular congregation are familiar with, as well as on the theme for the service. An ecumenical service, involving members of different denominations, may be more traditional because there is less material familiar to all the congregations represented. The suggestions in this section certainly are not exclusive – users of this book will probably come up with many more specific ideas for the themes they want to tackle. In the following list, each Bible reading has also been given a heading, to indicate how it might be used. These are, however, far from exhaustive or fully comprehensive.

OLD TESTAMENT

Genesis 3:1-15	Sin brings suffering because the relationship with God has been broken.
Genesis 4:1-12	Sin is always destructive.
Genesis 15:1-15	God's promise to Abram; the place of faith.
Genesis 21:14-21	God hears the cry of the rejected and unwanted.
Genesis 32:22-32	Wrestling with God.
Exodus 15:22-27	The Lord who heals us.
Exodus 23:1-9	Caring for others and acting fairly.
Numbers 20:1-13	The results of complaining and dissatisfaction.
Numbers 21:4-9	The bronze snake.
Deuteronomy 6:13-25	Obedience and following God brings blessing.
Ruth 1:8-18	Sadness at a difficult decision.
1 Samuel 1:1-20	Hannah's distress and prayer.
1 Samuel 28:3-20	The disastrous consequences of spiritism.
2 Samuel 9:1-11	Healing old wounds in relationships.
1 Kings 3:5-14	Solomon asking for wisdom.
2 Kings 4:15-37	A dead son restored to life.
2 Kings 5:1-14	Naaman healed of leprosy.
2 Kings 20:1-11	Hezekiah miraculously healed after prayer.
Nehemiah 5:1-13	Fair treatment for the weak and exploited.

Psalm 1	Meditating on God's Law.
Psalm 6	A prayer for healing.
Psalm 16	Joy in God's presence.
Psalm 23	Trusting in God's protection and guidance.
Psalm 27	Seeking God's face.
Psalm 30	Praise for God's healing.
Psalm 32	Healing and forgiveness.
Psalm 34	God our deliverer and saviour.
Psalm 37:1-11	Be still and wait for God.
Psalm 40:1-10	Praise for God's salvation.
Psalm 41	Trusting God for deliverance.
Psalm 51	A psalm of penitence.
Psalm 63	God satisfies our deepest needs.
Psalm 91	Resting in God.
Psalm 103	God is compassionate and loving.
Psalm 107:1-16	Trusting God to protect and help.
Psalm 147	Praising God for his healing power, even over sadness.
Proverbs 3:1-18	Wisdom brings healing.
Proverbs 15:1-18	Healing in relationships.
Isaiah 1:10-20	Spectacular worship is no substitute for showing others the love of God.
Isaiah 6:1-8	The prophet's vision of God's holiness, and awareness of his own sinfulness.
Isaiah 11:1-9	The Spirit of the Lord rests on the 'Branch from Jesse'.

Isaiah 12	A song of praise to God.
Isaiah 43:1-7	Do not be afraid.
Isaiah 51:1-8	Salvation for ever.
Isaiah 52:12-53:12	Healing comes through the Suffering Servant.
Isaiah 55:1-5/6-13	The Lord brings refreshment and joy to all who turn to him.
Isaiah 61	God's Spirit anoints the prophet to proclaim good news to all in need or pain.
Jeremiah 17:7-14	The prophet seeks healing in a time of adversity.
Jeremiah 30:17-22	The Lord promises to restore Zion to health.
Jeremiah 33:6-16	Healing for the nation.
Ezekiel 34:11-16	God will care for his flock himself.
Hosea 6:1-6/11:1-9	God longs to heal his people.
Hosea 14	God's anger is turned away.
Joel 2:18-27	God will restore the land.
Malachi 4	The day of the Lord will bring healing.

New Testament

Matthew 8:5-13	The centurion's faith.
Matthew 9:27-38	Healing and preaching the good news.
Matthew 15:21-28	The Syro-Phoenician woman's daughter is delivered from demon-possession.

Mark 2:1-12	The paralysed man brought to Jesus by his friends.
Mark 5:1-20	A demon-possessed man is healed.
Mark 9:14-29	The disciples cannot heal a demon-possessed lad.
Mark 10:46-52	Bartimaeus' sight is restored.
Luke 4:14-21	Jesus as the fulfilment of Isaiah's prophecy.
Luke 4:31-44	Jesus heals various conditions and preaches the good news of the kingdom.
Luke 6:1-11	Jesus heals on the Sabbath.
Luke 7:11-17	The widow's son raised from death.
Luke 8:40-56	Faith and healing.
Luke 9:1-6	The disciples sent out to heal.
Luke 10:1-12	The seventy-two commissioned to preach and heal.
Luke 11:14-28	Authority to heal.
Luke 15:11-32	The father who forgives.
Luke 17:11-19	Thanksgiving for healing.
Luke 19:1-10	Zaccheus made whole.
Luke 23:32-43	The dying thief accepted by Jesus.
John 4:43-54	The official's son healed.
John 5:1-15	Do you want to be healed?
John 9:1-12/13-34	The man whose sight was restored, and the issue of spiritual blindness.

John 10:11-16	The Good Shepherd who cares for his sheep.
John 11:17-44	Jesus the resurrection and the life.
John 14:1-14	Jesus' followers to continue his work.
John 15:1-12	Bearing fruit for Jesus the true vine.
Acts 3:1-16	Peter and John heal a lame beggar.
Acts 4:1-22	Peter and John give account for the healing.
Acts 4:23-31	The believers pray for the gift of the Holy Spirit.
Acts 5:12-16	The believers heal many.
Acts 8:9-23	Motives for healing.
Acts 20:7-12	Eutychus revived by Paul.
Acts 28:1-10	Malta experiences God's healing power.
1 Corinthians 12:1-11	Gifts from the Holy Spirit.
2 Corinthians 4:7 -18	God's power at work in us.
2 Corinthians 12:1-10	The thorn in the flesh.
Ephesians 6:10-20	The armour of God.
Hebrews 2:10-18	Jesus our great High Priest.
James 5:13-20	Praying in faith.
1 Peter 2:13-25	Suffering for Christ's sake and healed by his wounds.
1 John 1:5-10	Walking in the light.
1 John 4:13-21	Love and fear.
Revelation 21:1-7	No pain or suffering in heaven.

Hymns and Music

Music can make or break a service. Well and sensitively played it has a powerful effect on the atmosphere – poorly sung hymns and incompetently played instruments also have a powerful effect, if not the desired one! It is vital to ensure that the choice of hymns reflects not just the season but also the overall theme of the service. Similarly, any instrumental music must be sensitive to the occasion – a quiet and meditative ending can easily be ruined by a mighty chord from the organ. The following hymns are only a brief selection of the most familiar from a number of well-known books. Rather than being listed according to season, they are grouped only as traditional or contemporary. Most congregations and groups have their own favourites, but familiarity should not override aptness and relevance to the occasion. Everybody will have a favourite that has been omitted, but the selection is wide enough to give most congregations plenty of scope, whatever their tradition or inclination.

Traditional

A man there lived in Galilee
All ye who seek for sure relief
And can it be
As pants the hart
At even, 'ere the sun was set
Come, thou long-expected Jesus
Dear Lord and Father of mankind
Hail to the Lord's anointed
Hark the glad sound
Hark! the herald angels sing
How sweet the name of Jesus sounds
I heard the voice of Jesus say
Immortal love, for ever full
In heavenly love abiding
Jesus lives! Thy terrors now
Just as I am
Lord, l was blind
Lord Jesus think on me
Lord of all hopefulness
My song is love unknown
O for a thousand tongues
Once in royal David's city
O worship the Lord in the beauty of holiness
Praise, my soul, the King of heaven
Sing praise to God, who reigns above
Thine be the glory
Thou, Lord, haste given thyself for our healing
We sing the praise of him who died
With joy we meditate the grace
God of mercy, God of grace
Peace, perfect peace

Contemporary

Be still and know
Be still, for the presence of the Lord
For this purpose Christ was revealed
Give thanks with a grateful heart
Healing God, Almighty Father
I believe in Jesus
I give you all the honour
I receive you, O Spirit of love
It's your blood that cleanses me
Jesus, we celebrate your victory
Jesus, you are changing me
Make way, make way!
O let the Son of God enfold you
O Lord, your tenderness
Our confidence is in the Lord
My peace I give unto you
Peter and John went to pray
Praise you, Lord, for the wonder of your healing
Rejoice, rejoice!
Safe in the shadow
The King is among us
The price is paid
There is power in the name of Jesus
He was pierced for our transgressions
I come with joy
Lord Christ, who on thy heart didst bear
When I needed a neighbour
There in God's garden
God is love: let Heaven adore him
For the healing of the nations

SAMPLE SERVICE OUTLINES

ADVENT HEALING SERVICE

Non-eucharistic

INTRODUCTORY SENTENCE	Isaiah 58:8 *
HYMN	Hark the glad sound
CONFESSION & ABSOLUTION	Responsary for Advent *
RESPONSORIAL PRAISE	Isaiah 40 *
HYMN	Hail to the Lord's Anointed
FIRST READING	Isaiah 55
HYMN	Come, thou long expected Jesus
SECOND READING	Luke 4:31-44
SERMON	
INTERCESSIONS	For Advent *
HYMN	From heaven you came (the Servant King)
TIME OF PRAYER AND MINISTRY	
CONCLUDING PRAYER	For Advent *
HYMN	How lovely on the mountains (our God reigns)
BLESSING	

* Items to be found in the appropriate sections

LENT HEALING SERVICE

Eucharistic

INTRODUCTORY SENTENCE	Luke 18:13 *
HYMN	How sweet the name of Jesus sounds
CONFESSION & ABSOLUTION	Responsary for Lent *
RESPONSORIAL WORDS	From Psalm 34 *
COLLECT FOR THE DAY	
OLD TESTAMENT READING	Hosea 6:1-6
NEW TESTAMENT READING	1 John 4:13-21
HYMN	Meekness and Majesty
GOSPEL READING	Luke 15:11-32
SERMON	
INTERCESSIONS	For Lent *
PRAYER OF HUMBLE ACCESS	
THE PEACE	
OFFERTORY HYMN	With joy we meditate the grace
OFFERTORY PRAYER	
COMMUNION PRAYER	
LORD'S PRAYER	
BREAKING OF BREAD	
INVITATION TO THE TABLE	

DISTRIBUTION OF COMMUNION WITH PRAYER AND LAYING ON OF HANDS

PRAYER AFTER COMMUNION	For Lent *
BLESSING AND DISMISSAL	
HYMN	My song is love unknown

* Items to be found in the appropriate sections

Pentecost Healing Service

Introductory Sentence	1 Corinthians 12:8-9 *
Hymn	Come down, O love divine
Responsorial Praise	From Psalm 36 *
First Reading	Isaiah 11:1-9
Hymn	He that is in us is greater
Second Reading	Acts 4:23-31
Sermon	
Intercessions	For Pentecost *
Hymn	Holy Spirit, we welcome you
Confession and Absolution	Responsary for Pentecost *
Time of Prayer and Ministry	
Concluding Prayer	For Pentecost *
Hymn	O Thou, who camest from above
Blessing	

* Items to be found in the appropriate sections

FURTHER READING

Morris Maddocks   *The Christian Healing Ministry*
                    (SPCK 1981, 1990)

Francis MacNutt   *Healing* (Hodder and Stoughton, 1989)

John Richards   *The Question of Healing Services*
                    (Daybreak, 1989)

NOTES